ENTREPRENEURING

THE

10

COMMANDMENTS
for

BUILDING
A
GROWTH
COMPANY

THIRD EDITION

48° 44' 00"N

123° 15' 00"W · 122° 44' 00"W

Archipelago Publishing
Friday Harbor, Washington

48° 24' 00"N

P.O. Box 1249, Friday Harbor WA 98250 • 1 (800) 360-6166

ABOUT THE AUTHOR

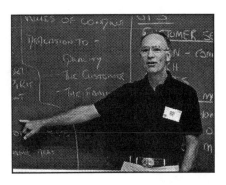

Steven C. Brandt is an experienced entrepreneur, company president, author, and faculty veteran of 21 years at the Stanford University Graduate School of Business in the heart of Silicon Valley. At Stanford he taught New Enterprises, Business Strategy, and Small Business Management to over 4,000 executives and MBAs during the '70s, '80s, and '90s. He has been a director of three public companies in or near Silicon Valley—a semiconductor company, a solar products company, and a bank. He has also been the co-founder/president of four different businesses in a range of industries including software, educational products, food, and sports services. Brandt has been a direct participant in the development of over twenty other new enterprises involved in everything from sailboats and biotechnology to music and artificial intelligence. The author, who has BSME, MBA, and PhD degrees, has written two other popular business books—*Focus Your Business: Strategic Planning in Emerging Companies*, and *Entrepreneuring in Established Companies*. He has a new video series entitled, *Managing the Emerging Company*. As the CEO of one NASDAQ-listed company puts it: Brandt is "...succinct and practical. He displays a rare combination of real-world experience, academic discipline, and humor." Today the author lives in a small community where he continues to develop materials for building businesses. Locally he is a hospital district commissioner and a land trust board member.

TABLE OF CONTENTS

For my wife, Wooly,
and the vital new crop of entrepreneurs
breaking out around the world . . .

Introduction

This book is written to be used. Entrepreneurship has undergone a renaissance in America that is echoing around the world. Terms like innovation and startup are already part of everyday conversation in most emerging countries. Seers write of a renaissance boosted by the Internet that will rival the agricultural and industrial revolutions which fueled much of our present-day, material prosperity. Venture capitalists are now featured regularly in the business press. IPOs (Initial Public Offerings) have grown from a rate of $0.6 Billion in 1970 to $1.4 B in 1980, $16.3 B in 1991, and $29.0 B in 1995. Engineers, out-placed managers, latent inventors, ambitious dropouts, blocked executives, tentative scientists, and MBAs frustrated with consulting or Wall Street find they can no longer suppress the itch to "just do it" as predictions and fears give way to the fact of turbulent times. They accurately sense that the timing for scratching the itch is as good as it is ever going to be.

Peaceful turbulence favors entrepreneuring, and as the 1990s slip by like clouds, there is plenty of opportunity. The trick is to take advantage of it, and history will show that in the decade ahead, most of the psychic and financial prizes will once again have gone to the bright and the bold who systematically generated fresh services, products, and experiences for discrete segments of our increasingly pluralistic society. Entrepreneuring is a cramped way of life in static times.

This book is not based on any romantic premise that everyone should be his or her own boss. This book *is* based on the premise that an increasingly well-educated, healthy, and environmentally-conscious population will stimulate and support a continuing flow of new industrial and consumer business opportunities that are compatible with the worldwide realities of the times. Those realities include population dynamics, an upheaval in communications, falling barriers to entry in many industries, economic gyrations, floating exchange rates, and a world where each country jostles with most others for the available gold rings. For many people, these realities are problems, or at least challenges. For entrepreneurs, they are possibilities in disguise. As one sage put it, "entrepreneuring ain't for the faint-of-heart."

In the pages that follow I have tried to present in a readable and usable fashion ten main *operating* principles for starting and building a company. Several caveats are in order. First, the Ten Commandments are aimed at people involved with growth companies, i.e. companies with founders and/or managers intent on building a bigger enterprise, hopefully much bigger! I have little experience with the wonderful world of boutiques, small-scale consulting, or family restaurants. Such enterprises, typically based on very personalized service, add spice to the times and will probably flourish in the years ahead. Power to them. I can only say that I did not have them specifically in mind as I fashioned the Ten Commandments out of my own failures, successes, so-sos, and observations during the last thirty years.

A second caveat is that the contents of this book are aimed at what I consider to be the mainline operating issues. No attempt is made to even touch upon the myriad other important matters connected with launching a successful enterprise and staying out of court or jail due to indiscretions pertaining to withholding taxes, partners, stockholders, spouses, customers, or employees. There is a wealth of information available on what is generally called small business management. Sources as diverse as the SBA, your local bank, trade associations, well-meaning institutes, countless college professors, and your local attorney annually pump out scores of pamphlets, books, and seminars on what I consider to be the administrative side of entrepreneuring. Make no mistake, administrative issues such as incorporation mechanics, filing for licenses, and obtaining workman's compensation insurance are vital. Treat them lightly only at your peril. This book, however, is not your source for guidance on administrative matters. Competent insurance people, attorneys, and accountants who have verifiable experience with successful young enterprises are what you need. Check their references.

The final caveat is that the Ten Commandments, even followed to the letter, will not automatically make you rich, beautiful, handsome, fulfilled, or whatever. I wish it could be otherwise, but the record indicates that the primary requirements for success are an identifiable and receptive market, a better mousetrap, sufficient capital, a balanced team to lead the way, tenacity, and thoughtful timing (some people call it luck). The Ten Commandments do aim to help you weave these ingredients together in a pragmatic way and to avoid some of the more common operating mistakes entrepreneurs tend to make during the early years when their young companies lack momentum and are still vulnerable to sudden failure from stockholder squabbles, unclear objectives, a short-term negative cash flow, or a shortage of functional talent.

Organized or institutionalized entrepreneurship is a relatively new phenomenon. Seminars and college courses on the subject have only begun to be offered on a regular basis in the last decade or so. Venture capital is just now gravitating to a position of legitimacy as a full-time, professional occupation of importance to the nation. Some people in government are taking note that new business formation is not just an academic idea but, in fact, the major proven and sustaining source of new jobs. Capital gains is enjoying a resurgence of respectability again. And technology is increasingly thought to be the United States' number one economic weapon in a tough competitive world. These are heady times for both declared and still undecided entrepreneurs. The commandments can help you think about the fundamentals for building a company.

Commandments One, Two, and Three cover key startup issues: Who should be involved? What are you out to accomplish? Who is going to buy what you are selling? Answers to these questions can save many a false start and point the way to creating a rock-like foundation for your new enterprise . . . if it's justified.

Commandment Four includes a Guide to Preparing a Business Plan. If you wish to build a business of any complexity at all, you should have a written plan. If you wish to attract outside money from people other than your friends and relatives, you must have a written plan. If you want to maximize your chances for building a viable, moneymaking enterprise without ruining your health in the process, you will have a written plan that has been critiqued by competent individuals whose opinions you respect.

Commandments Five through Eight deal with day-to-day operating matters that confront the senior people attempting to implement a written plan for building a business. Staffing, rewarding, extending the company, and paying the bills as you go are like blocking, passing, running, and tackling in football. The team that executes well will tend to win its share of games.

Finally, Commandments Nine and Ten are aimed at salting entrepreneuring with a modicum of professionalism. The term professionalism denotes objectivity and detachment in the vocational matters at hand. Entrepreneurship has long and properly been associated with sweat equity, an unyielding dedication that often leads to a merging of the identities of the founder(s) and the enterprise itself. Such a merging sometimes makes for certain efficiencies, but it almost always limits a growth company over the longer run. The entrepreneur has but two choices when his or her enterprise successfully grows: either change and grow with it or stop succeeding. Knowing when and how to change requires at least a half-an-arm's-length relationship with the budding business entity itself. The company is the company; you are you. They are not the same entity. Working from a proper business plan (Commandment Four) can help maintain this separation.

Just a few last words on philosophy. I have long thought that entrepreneuring was a lifestyle choice, and most of the high-rise company founders, officers, and venture capitalists who have contributed to the ideas in this book have tended to confirm this thought. The 1970s formula was for an entrepreneur to start something, build it up, sell out, get out, and start the cycle again. But I think now that a new day is dawning. The 1990s breed of entrepreneur tends to be part of an entrepreneurial team that sticks with the ship and, more importantly, keeps on innovating. This does not in any way diminish the need and opportunity for the classic soloist; it just enlarges the doorway to the legitimate entrepreneur's club.

It's a fine club. Entrepreneuring is a spirited way of life. These Ten Commandments are aimed at expanding the membership.

Steven C. Brandt
Friday Harbor,
Washington USA

Picking Business Partners

THE FIRST COMMANDMENT

> LIMIT THE NUMBER OF PRIMARY PARTICIPANTS TO PEOPLE WHO CAN CONSCIOUSLY AGREE UPON AND CONTRIBUTE DIRECTLY TO THAT WHICH THE ENTERPRISE IS TO ACCOMPLISH, FOR WHOM, AND BY WHEN.

There are many reasons people become involved in young, growing companies as owners, investors, or key employees. The broad range of satisfactions sought runs from an opportunity for personal expression on one end of the spectrum to capital gains on the other. Unless there is compatibility between what the primary participants want out of the business, debilitating conflict is likely to ensue. The process of trying to reach conscious agreement on the purpose of the enterprise is often difficult and revealing.

The primary participants in a young enterprise are those people who share the initial ownership and/or management decision-making processes. The early months and years in the life of a company are critical ones in which the tone and shape of the venture are determined. If the character formed during the early days is convoluted by too much compromise or scarred by too much acrimonious debate, the foundation upon which the business is to be built will be less sturdy than it could and should be.

Here is a list of six common mistakes that would-be entrepreneurs often make in piecing together participants at the start of a new venture:

- The founding group is formed spontaneously.
- Personal or family lawyers, insurance agents, CPAs, and bankers are automatically used as advisers.
- Harmony is sought at the expense of creative conflict.
- Needed support people are given stock or stock options before they have proven their likely, long-term value.
- The board of directors consists solely or primarily of insiders—company officers, their spouses, and friends or relatives.
- People with widely varying motives are mixed together in the same financial lifeboat.

Let's consider these six common mistakes in a bit more depth.

The founding group is formed spontaneously. It doesn't take a novelist to portray a buzzing weekend cocktail party or an animated, after-work conversation in a car or café during which a new product or service or distribution idea suddenly materializes and grows wings. It's a euphoric moment, and the two, three, or more souls standing in the circle are each caught up in the conception. Too often, they are also included willy-nilly as investors or key employees in the new venture.

The spontaneous combination of souls may be just what the venture needs; then again, it may not be. The choice of investors and staff ideally should flow from a thorough understanding of the requirements for success in the prospective business. Essentially random collections of folks seldom make the right bedfellows for business building even if they are coworkers, classmates, or professional cousins.

How does an entrepreneur go about exploring an idea and triggering enthusiasm and interest, while at the same time reaching the ideal of limiting the number of primary participants to those who can consciously agree upon and contribute directly to that which the enterprise is to accomplish? *Cautiously* is perhaps the best advice. The proper mindset is one that says that the eventual blueprint for building the business–the Business Plan–will dictate the desired specifications for investors and staff alike. If a small, qualified group can be organized to create the blueprint with a clear understanding from the start that everyone may not make the construction team if the bid is won, then the spontaneity risk is at least addressed.

Here is an illustration of how Commandment One was violated via an incompatibility of interests in the founding group.

CASE A. A bright, energetic high school dropout conceived a new athletic shoe for the jogger market. He told and sold his uncle, an accountant, on the concept. Together they raised close to $100,000 from individual outside investors, mostly friends who were avid joggers.

The $100,000 represented essentially all the capital put into the company. The shoe was introduced to the local market and sold very well. The company became a regional success story. The outside investors wanted to keep the earnings in the business and expand it. The founder/president wanted to play with new shoe designs, do research and de-
(case continued on next page)

---

velopment, and give speeches on entrepreneurship at lun-
cheon-club meetings. The uncle/general manager was happy
taking home $50,000 a year (his salary), and he didn't want
to travel very far to build the business. The company quickly
stagnated and eventually faltered. No one won. The founder
lost his hero status; the uncle, his interesting job; the investors, their money. Each participant had his or her eye on a
different star: that which the enterprise is to accomplish, for
whom.

Common mistake number two has to do with guidance on administrative matters.

**Personal or family lawyers, insurance agents,
CPAs, and bankers are automatically used as advisers.** Growth companies don't just happen. There is a
lot of administrative expertise needed to glue the pieces
together and keep the enterprise on a peaceful course
among the snags and shoals of government requirements
and legal practice. Any average attorney, CPA, or insurance agent can speak the language, give you advice, mail
you something to sign, and send a bill. Not many have
the professional interest and proven experience to help
you build a business. It's a relatively narrow spectrum
of practice. An entrepreneur has enough to do without in-
vesting time and money in his or her advisers' educations!

In every major metropolitan area there are CPAs,
attorneys, and insurance people who have developed or
are developing a reputation with embryonic companies.
Seek them out. Interview them. Discuss fees. Check their
references. Then select who you want and listen to what
he or she has to say. Your job as a modern entrepreneur
is not to have all the answers, but to know where to get
them. How to insure that you ask the right questions is
covered later in this chapter.

Now what about bankers? In general, most of them do not have particular, in-depth expertise in business building. However, with the trend toward deregulation, some are learning out of necessity. Good bankers know about money, particularly debt money. And in Commandment Eight you will be advised to cultivate *all* your potential money sources on a continuing basis. So developing a working relationship with a reputable banker can be useful. But don't confuse doing so with developing a workable financial plan for your new enterprise. For a comprehensive financial plan you need assistance from one or more persons skilled in corporate finance–particularly start-up and small business financing. For example, investment bankers, venture capitalists, and occasionally business school professors of finance or accounting may be helpful. Someone who has worked the numbers and lived through a start-up or two in the same or nearly the same industry as your own is probably the best single source of guidance.

Harmony is sought at the expense of creative conflict. Entrepreneurs by nature tend to listen most attentively to themselves. In today's competitive world, as a gesture toward open-mindedness, however, they may well seek the counsel of others. But there is a human tendency to hear mostly what you want to hear. "Yes, Steve, you are right. There is a *huge,* untapped market for your widgets." Experience indicates, however, that bad or negative news will cost you or me a lot less if we get it sooner rather than later.

The primary participants in a new enterprise should bring a balanced, thoughtful view to the decision-making process. This precludes yes-people as well as those unqualified to make a direct contribution to the matters at hand.

CASE B. A group of three prominent, academic scientists spotted a major opportunity in the emerging bio-medical industry. Technically it was within their combined spheres of expertise. They mulled over the opportunity for nearly a year and then happened onto a young MBA student with no bio-med experience in search of a field project for one of his classes. The student developed for them an elaborate business plan with computer-generated projections covering every conceivable scenario. The four people got along well together in both business and social settings. The projections looked good. Four months later, seed financing was obtained from an overseas venture capital firm and the MBA was hired as the general manager of the newly formed company. Everyone was euphoric.

Now ask yourself: How reliable are the projections? Recall, they were developed for the scientists by a busy student who needed a job after graduation. How well qualified is the new general manager to build a competitive bio-med company around the scientists' skills? How could some creative conflict have been beneficially woven into the formative period of this potential growth company?

Needed support people are given stock or stock options before they have proven their likely, long-term value. Cash is almost always tight in the early days of a new enterprise. Among other things, cash is needed to attract people who can turn the wheels to produce positive cash flow...to pay the people! It is a chicken or egg problem. The practical question that often pops up is: How can we attract (and motivate) people with a minimum cash outlay? Too often the answer is: Spread some stock or options around in lieu of cash. It's a bad answer.

Here are a few of the reasons why. Stock can get into the hands of people you later have to release. So you end up with some angry stockholders/owners. Stock can get into the hands of people whom professional investors you could otherwise attract during future rounds of financing would consider to be unacceptable equity partners. Stock spread around may well come back to the company via a repurchase option at exactly the point in time when the company can least afford to buy back shares, such as when the company or the economy is in a dip. And sometimes shares (and, of course, people) on the loose end up in your competitors' camps, which might on occasion compromise your operation.

Does this mean that there is no room at all for stock or options for support people involved in a start-up? The best answer is a qualified yes. Until the enterprise has some stability—has passed permanently beyond the point of negative cash flow, for instance—restrict the ownership risks and potential rewards to the primary participants who, by definition, are making a unique, direct contribution. And beyond the point of initial stability, issue stock to secondary company builders only after giving the matter deep, detailed, long-term thought. Stock certificates worth less than the buyer paid for them or that are dropping in book value aren't exactly instruments of motivation.

CASE C. A young entrepreneur had an idea: Build a bungee-jump tower at a ski area so skiers could add to their winter fun. He sold the idea and forty percent of the new company to an investor who put up the money to build the tower. He also sold a significant amount of stock at the founder's price to a buddy who agreed to help operate the tower. Two years later, bungee sales were good but below projections. The investor wanted out and the buddy wanted to leave the snow country for good. The entrepreneur now had unhappy shareholders who owned over half of "his" company, and he was short on cash to buy either one of them out. He had a dilemma, at best!

The board of directors consists solely or primarily of insiders–company officers, their spouses, and friends or relatives. Legal matters aside, the operating purpose of a board is to aid, abet, challenge, and replace, as necessary, the chief executive officer (CEO) of the enterprise in pursuit of the stockholders' interests. Those interests are generally financial (fiduciary) in nature, so a growth company board ideally concentrates on helping the CEO optimize the financial performance of the company over some finite period of time. If the CEO/entrepreneur is open to seasoned advice (see "creative conflict" above), he or she is unlikely to get it–at least anything very powerful–from insiders, spouses, friends, or relatives. A properly constituted board can inexpensively double the width of a young company's management's point of view. One or two directors with the right experience base can add up to a whole additional, sound, primary participant. A strong board can be your single best source of the right questions as the enterprise learns first to stand, and then to walk...and run.

People with widely varying motives are mixed together in the same financial lifeboat. A huge spectrum of people participate in small, growing companies. Some of them are seeking long-term capital gains; they understand that it usually takes stock to really build one's own net worth. Other people are after a comfortable annual income. Still others are primarily interested in technical challenge and its tributaries–problem solving, personal expression, and, perhaps, fame. The smart entrepreneur will illuminate the driving force in each of his or her potential colleagues and think hard about whether there is compatibility across the basic team.

It is completely honorable for a group of talented people to join together to build a company with the intention to give each participant a chance to do his or her own thing and, incidentally, make a buck in the process. Problems arise, however, if responsible outside investors are brought into the same company under the false pretenses that management intends to vigorously grow the enterprise and enrich everyone including the investors in a fixed number of years.

In summary, Commandment One is important because a new company is an egg shell. It needs a well-developed internal system of supports and braces to withstand the pressures of entering and competing successfully in a marketplace. Appropriate supports and braces can be conceived and squeezed into place by dedicated people with qualifications especially suited to the configuration of the particular egg. The entrepreneur faces the task of gathering just the right number of right people. Too few result in weakness; too many create chaos; and the wrong ones produce dissension.

What Business Are You In?

THE SECOND COMMANDMENT

DEFINE THE BUSINESS OF THE ENTERPRISE IN TERMS OF WHAT IS TO BE BOUGHT, PRECISELY BY WHOM, AND WHY.

Businesses are organs of society that perform tasks associated with providing most goods and services the public decides it wishes to own and use. Under this capitalistic system, a business can prosper to the extent that it performs its particular tasks effectively and efficiently within the law. The nature of the tasks to be performed usually changes over time as those served change. The people in a successful company predict and respond to their chosen customers' needs. Customers, therefore, define an enduring business. At all times, some customers are growing in their ability to buy; others are declining. The astute manager ascertains which is which.

Over thirty years ago, Ted Levitt published an article entitled, *Marketing Myopia**, which is still influencing the way a lot of business people think about their world. Levitt pointed out that customers buy need satisfactions, not products. He illustrated his point with two famous examples of business myopia. Why did the railroads of the nation, once very prosperous, growth businesses, fall from grace? Because railroad business people persisted too long in selling their product, railbound movement, and failed to recognize that customers were buying *transportation*. Transportation was the generic need being satisfied, and when new forms like airplanes, trucks, and cars came along, there was no reluctance among railroad customers to switch to them. Had railroad managements been less myopic, they would have led the way into new forms of transportation.

A similar story emanated from the movie industry. What were people buying when they went to the movies? The movie business people of the 1940s assumed the answer was movies, of course. Levitt noted that a more useful view would have been that people were buying *entertainment*. If movie people had focused on the generic need for entertainment, they might have been the first into the new medium of television when it appeared. The same kind of question can be asked today of bankers. Do consumers want banking? Or do they want help with money *transactions*? Once upon a time, banks were about the only source of help with transactions. This is not the case any more.

Entrepreneurs face three related occupational hazards. First, they tend to concentrate too heavily upon what they have to sell and too lightly upon what is being bought—the myopia problem outlined above. This is a particularly prevalent hazard with engineers, scientists, and inventors who, almost by definition, are likely to be deeply entwined with their product or process.

*Theodore Levitt, "Marketing Myopia," *Harvard Business* Review, July-August, 1960, p. 45.

Second, entrepreneurs tend to generalize about who the real customers are. "Companies" and "consumers" are extremely vague classes of potential buyers. Finally, entrepreneurs in their enthusiasm and infectious optimism sometimes fail to pinpoint the reasons why a given, individual decision maker might buy the entrepreneur's specific new product, service, or experience. "Because it's better," lacks something in terms of precision.

Following are three short cases to illuminate these hazards to a successful startup operation.

CASE D. Two technical (electromechanical) people left a major west coast instrument manufacturer to cofound a teaching machine company. The product, an audiovisual-response device, worked well and seemed to have a number of potential applications. Consider the dictates of Commandment Two and think about these three questions.

1. What might customers buy from the new company?
2. Who might make the buying decisions?
3. Why might various types of buyers buy the machine?
   –Think about the answers before proceeding–

Here is a partial list of possible answers to the questions.
Q1. Customers might buy teaching machines to:
   Reduce teacher or instructor costs
   Improve student or trainee retention of material
   Increase efficiency (teach more people per hour)
   Improve utilization of facilities
   Help slow learners
Q2. The buying decision might be made by:
   Academic Market Segment
   | Teachers | School administrators |
   | School board | PTAs |
   Business/Industrial Market Segment
   | Profit center managers | Training directors |
   | Personnel managers | Purchasing agents |
Q3. A given buyer might buy in order to:
   Improve his or her performance
   Enhance his or her reputation as an innovator
   Capture available investment tax credits before they expire
   Experiment
   Avoid hiring additional people

There are certainly a lot of possibilities! Effective entrepreneuring requires that the possibilities be reduced in number to the point where rifle-shot marketing and selling becomes possible.

CASE E. A famous tennis champion started a chain of tennis camps. Initially he had summer camps for children. Then he began expanding to week-long and weekend programs for adults. Essentially the same marketing, advertising, and operations approach was used for both segments of the tennis camp market—children and adults. The venture into the adult market failed. Commandment Two was violated.

	Children Camps	Adult Camps
What is bought?		
	1. Tennis skills	1. Social mixing
	2. Camp experience	2. Vacation
	3. "Baby"-sitting	3. Tennis skills
Who buys?	Parents	Adults—mostly singles
Why?	1. Child development	1. New experience
	2. Social status	2. Physical fitness
	3. Free-up time during school vacation	3. Athletic prowess
		4. Meet opposite sex

In Case E, properly defining the business in terms of its customers would have led the entrepreneur to the conclusion that, in fact, he was dealing with at least two discrete tennis businesses. Each business had its own distinct marketing and operations requirements for success.

CASE F. Several physicians teamed up to take advantage of the opportunity they saw to use computers in hospitals. They pulled together an extraordinarily sharp group of programmers and systems people and developed packages for a va-

(case continued on next page)

riety of applications. The physician/entrepreneurs produced a large, handsomely-bound business plan. One seasoned investor made these notes on the cover after a detailed reading of the plan: "I can't tell if you are intending to sell a) time-savings to doctors, b) cost savings to hospital administrators due to possibly fewer nurses per floor or ward, c) greater revenue to accounting people due to tighter controls on miscellaneous charges, or d) shorter hospital stays to patients and insurance companies." The potential investor said no to the investment opportunity.

Of course, if an entrepreneuring team such as the one in Case F has enough money, it may be able to muddle through the range of alternatives and eventually ferret out one or more solid, profit-making opportunities. There is almost always going to be some muddling, which is why a young company needs an adequate supply of money up front, i.e., capitalization. But there is a lot to be said for minimizing the muddle factor beforehand with hard thought, market research, field interviews, and actual sales calls. Up to some point short of paralysis by analysis, the respective enterprise should be defined as tightly as possible on paper. This doesn't preclude deviations in direction based on new information later on. It may, however, help you avoid spending a lot of energy and money only to find that there's no there, there!

CASE G. An adult student and later friend of the tennis champion in Case E above conceived and developed a videotape device. It was designed to allow tennis pros, and perhaps ski school pros, to record students' motions and play them back with stop action and other diagnostic features. The engineer/entrepreneur, the champ, and everyone who saw themselves played back on the screen bubbled with enthusiasm. Money was raised easily for a new venture based

(case continued on next page)

on the device and production was inaugurated amid appropriate fanfare. After all, how could a champ be wrong? The
company expected to sell 1000-2000 units at around $4000
each the first year, a projection based on selling units to a
what the entrepreneur thought was a "reasonable" percentage of the number of teaching pros, racquet clubs, etc., across
the country. The fledgling company sold a grand total of
twenty-three units nationwide during its first year in business.

What went wrong? Very simple. Tennis pros generally saw—and still see—themselves as artists. They didn't
need diagnostic devices, particularly ones that were cum-
bersome and required maintenance. In addition, many
of them didn't care much for the champ who was featured prominently in the advertisements. And finally,
neither the teaching pros nor the clubs that provided
the courts had much spending money.

The world of interest to the entrepreneur is filled
with individuals who have some amount of change in
their, or their companies', pockets. The most basic business transaction occurs when an individual exchanges
his or her change for whatever it is you, the builder of a
business, are selling. If there are enough individuals
willing to make such an exchange at a price that allows
you to pay your way and have enough left over to make
the effort and risk worthwhile, then you may have a case
for proceeding with a new enterprise. Otherwise, don't.
If you are unsure, tiptoe until you can assemble enough
hard data from customers—purchase orders, letters of
intent, survey results, field tests—to justify a go decision. Getting balanced input from others qualified to
entrepreneur with you (Commandment One) and ago-
nizing through the preparation of a business plan
(Commandment Four) can help you sort through and
rationalize the maze of options that confronts the people
who lead a new enterprise.

Focus, Focus, Focus

THE THIRD COMMANDMENT

CONCENTRATE ALL AVAILABLE RESOURCES ON ACCOMPLISHING TWO OR THREE SPECIFIC OPERATIONAL OBJECTIVES WITHIN A GIVEN TIME PERIOD.

Enterprises have finite resources. A smaller company achieves competitive advantage when playing for limited, explicit gains in a marketplace of its own choosing. Specialization breeds an organization sensitive to opportunities and quick to act. But any advantage withers if follow through is weak. It will be weak if resources are dissipated. Resource dilution is a sure formula for mediocrity, a state of being that aspiring growth businesses cannot afford.

MBO (Managing by Objectives) has been a popular phrase since the 1960s when the acronym and practice were gradually assimilated into the inventory of management techniques. In effect, when working with objectives, an entrepreneur or manager determines what he or she wants to accomplish, by when, and sets out to reach that objective. The individual involved focuses on the end result and tries to make it happen. The alternative, working without objectives, causes an individual to focus on day-to-day *activities*, to work hard and hope everything turns out all right.

There are four major variations on how to manage a business *without* using objectives:

Managing by Extrapolation (MBE)

Users of this system keep on doing what they have always done. More is normally merrier, and over time all lines on the planning chart move upward and to the right. This essentially historical approach was adequate during the first half of this century because of the latent demand for products and services as the population in the United States grew in size and nature from a largely rural society to an almost completely urban one. Car companies and their suppliers produced and distributed cars; radio companies made radios; banks handled money; and so forth. Even after World War II, business was in a relatively steady state in which tomorrow could reasonably be expected to look a lot like yesterday. The primary task for top managers was to do the same things right–that is, more efficiently. A look at the national productivity curve during the 1960s and 1970s shows that, in total, business managements succeeded in doing *things right*. In the 1990s, attention has been shifted to doing only certain things, the *right things,* through processes such as strategic planning and downsizing.

Managing by Crisis (MBC)

This system, long the specialty of the entrepreneur, has picked up a larger following in recent times for two reasons. First, business life is much more complex than it used to be. Thus there are more crises to be handled. Second, there are a great many more technical people in positions of management responsibility today. As a group they tend to be great problem solvers. Give them a crisis and they will smother it with energy and innovation. Should there be a gap in the flow of problems, chances are good that one can be invented—something nice and tangible that a manager can get his or her arms around, or teeth into. Management by crisis is popular. At the end of any given day, no one can say the boss didn't earn his or her pay!

Managing by Subjectives (MBS)

A dictionary definition of the word, subjective, is: *. . .existing or originating within the observer's mind or sense organs and, hence, incapable of being checked externally or being verified by other persons.*

As the cat said to Alice as she hesitated along the path to Wonderland, if you don't know where you are going, any road will take you there. There are companies that operate successfully this way, i.e., with very few people knowing where they are going. Everyone does the best he or she can to accomplish what he or she thinks *should* be done. Somewhere up in the organization there is presumed to be a guiding star. And there could well be. As long as a given business lends itself to masterminding or central processing by a single individual or a small team, implementation is relatively straightforward and not much talent is needed below the top level.

People just do what they are told to do. MBS can work as long as the business is simple. For an emerging company, however, which attracts complexity like a magnet, MBS can be a real limitation.

In particular, a subjective approach to building a business is unlikely to attract and hold the caliber of people required to capitalize on a competitive advantage. Good people want to know: Where are we headed? How are we doing? How am I doing? And so on. Few new enterprises do more than one thing really well. Attention should be focused on what that one thing is and what results are expected. The presence of overriding business objectives can serve as a rallying point, if people know what they are, because people tend to rise to meet expectations they understand.

Managing by Hope (MBH)

Most readers over forty years old recognize that the pace of life in the corporate world has increased markedly in recent years. Business decisions, such as staffing, capital investments, and new services, to name just a few, seem to have more ramifications than before. Certainties are hard to find. The uncertainties of the times have led some management teams into willy-nilly diversification in the hope that going in several directions at once will work out. The same uncertainties have led other management teams into bureaucratic analysis in the vain hope that something will turn up to point the way for the enterprise. MBH is, essentially, a form of reacting rather than acting, of letting events control you rather than vice versa. It is the other end of the spectrum from MBO, managing by objectives.

For those serious about entrepreneuring, a sound operational objective is one that is *measurable, dated,* and *vital* as a stepping stone, at a given point in time.

For example, for any given week or month or quarter or year, objectives could be formulated in the areas of sales volume, profitability, cash flow, staffing, product development, production, or margin improvement. Business judgment, based on a combination of facts, advice, and intuition can guide people on the entrepreneuring trail in the process of setting objectives. Creative conflict among the primary participants should ideally lead to agreement on the measures to be taken, by when, and and also on the accountability of whoever "owns" each objective.

Exercise

PART I.

Picture a startup company in which three cofounders have left their previous jobs, scraped together $50,000 from personal sources, and spent four months working day and night designing a new device that they think will revolutionize the way paper labels are applied to cans and bottles by food and beverage companies. As the trio completes its fourth month, the product prototype clearly works in the shop–a garage, naturally. At a Saturday morning meeting the entrepreneurs congratulate themselves on coming so far. "We did it!" They then properly turn their thoughts to, What next? They discuss a number of areas in which objectives could be set. Possible objectives are formulated and listed on a four-by-eight-foot piece of plywood which has the company name, Widgetronics, Inc., carefully lettered across the top.

Please examine the list that follows and decide which of the ten objectives are sound as stated by the entrepreneurs.

Sound?   Yes   No

1. Field test the prototype.   ___ ___
2. Obtain some orders.   ___ ___
3. Prepare a business plan.   ___ ___
4. Identify, interview, and hire a bookkeeper.   ___ ___
5. Line up more money by end of quarter.   ___ ___
6. Get minimum of 1,000 full-load hours on each
    of three devices by September 30.
    (Keep detailed maintenance log.)   ___ ___
7. Obtain two firm purchase orders for trial
    installations by October 31.   ___ ___
8. Draft a twelve-month plan and submit to
    Board by August 15.   ___ ___
9. Add a part-time bookkeeper no later than end
    of quarter.   ___ ___
10. Contact enough potential investors before
    September Board meeting to find at least three
    interested in Widgetronics.   ___ ___

To repeat an earlier statement, a sound objective for a new enterprise is one that is *measurable, dated,* and *vital* at that point in time. How many of the ten objectives shown above are sound as stated?

Given our criteria, only the last five of the above objectives are sound. The first five are pleasant statements of good intentions or ideas. Numbers six through ten, however, have some bite and lend themselves to accountability. By September 30 did someone specific get a minimum of 1000 full-load hours on each of three machines? With such an objective, someone can succeed or fail, be rewarded or reprimanded, and keep his or her eye on the right ball, in a manner of speaking. When an entrepreneuring team has a small, coordinated set of smart objectives, the chances of moving a company successfully from nothing to something are vastly improved.

What are "smart" objectives?

Exercise
PART II.

Here are objectives numbered six through ten from the list above:

6. *Get minimum of 1,000 full-load hours on each of three devices by September 30. (Keep detailed maintenance log.)*
7. *Obtain two firm purchase orders for trial installations by October 31.*
8. *Draft a twelve-month plan & submit to Board by August 15.*
9. *Add a part-time bookkeeper no later than end of quarter.*
10. *Contact enough potential investors before September Board meeting to find at least three interested in Widgetronics.*

Assume it is early August and you are advising the Widgetronics founders on what they should concentrate on next. Further assume that for some good and sufficient reason the Widgetronic management team has decided it will formally adopt a maximum of two operational objectives for the next phase of the business. Which two of the six would you recommend?

Hard to say, isn't it? From the limited information on Widgetronics available to you it is very difficult to decide what is most vital to the health of the enterprise in the fourth month of its first year. Arguments can be advanced for completing the product testing, getting a solid order or two, laying out a plan, adding staff to keep the paperwork in order, and cultivating investors. There will also always be a compelling argument for doing everything at once! However, doing, or trying to do, everything at once is a common failing of entrepreneurs. The only practical safeguard is the active presence of one or two primary participants with the desired dedication to managing with objectives. As stated at the start of this chapter in the exposition immediately following Commandment Three, *Resource dilution is a sure formula for mediocrity...*

Why only two operational objectives for Widgetronics? There's nothing magic about two. Why not one, or perhaps three—one per founder? The point is that it should be a small number. When everybody does everything, nothing gets done well. When everybody concentrates on just one or two prime results, there is a good chance those prime results will be achieved. And, there's normally room for getting some other things done, too. The task is to make sure the other things don't detract from accomplishing the prime ones.

There are many distractions in entrepreneuring. For example, there are a lot of fun things to do such as design letterheads, pick out offices, visit the printer, go to service club luncheons, and drop by the bank. There are a lot of satisfying and comfortable things to do, too, comfortable in that you have done them well in the past. For example, you may feel really good about product engineering, working in the plant, selling, hustling investors, or whatever. It's easy to use up the lion's share of your time doing what you do best, whether or not it is what the the business really needs at the moment. And then there are the often, less-than-pleasant new challenges such as producing quality goods without the right tools; cold-calling on potential customers who have never heard of you, your company, or your spectacular new service; phoning a venture capitalist for the umpteenth time to see if he or she has even read your business plan yet; and taking prospective key employees to dinner with your own money. How does an effective entrepreneur go about making the right trade-off decisions between the different calls on his or her finite time? There's no formula, but experience indicates that having crisp, agreed-upon objectives helps one avoid distractions and focus on what is vital.

Preparing a Business Plan

THE FOURTH COMMANDMENT

PREPARE AND WORK FROM A
WRITTEN PLAN THAT DELINEATES
WHO IN THE TOTAL ORGANIZATION
IS TO DO WHAT, BY WHEN.

*Until committed to paper, intentions are seeds
without soil, sails without wind, mere wishes which
render communication within an organization
inefficient, understanding uncertain, feedback
inaccurate, and execution sporadic. Without
execution, there is no payoff. The process of
committing plans to paper is easy to postpone under
the press of day-to-day events. In the absence of a
document, fully coordinated usage of the resources
of the business is unlikely. Each participant travels
along a different route toward a destination of his
or her own choosing. Decisions are made
independently, without a map. Time is lost, energy
squandered.*

"Getting it down on paper seemed to help." This captures the verdict that many, if not most, successful entrepreneurs reach *after* they have toiled through the process of preparing a business plan either for a startup or for the coming year in an ongoing enterprise. But *before* such plans are put to paper, far too many business builders think, "I'm busy—I'll get to it later." Why is this so? Most people can write well enough. Why do people hesitate to commit to paper what is in their heads?

The answer is complex, but it boils down to this: What is consciously in an entrepreneur's head is usually not as complete, as good, or as promising as he or she would like to think it is. He or she may have an image but it is a long way from being a finished painting. Or, to use a different metaphor, the entrepreneur may have a melody, but it is not yet a symphony. The process of getting an idea down on paper in a business plan format can be a very creative one. It is not merely a matter of translation from head to paper, but of actually generating the complete original. This is typically a heavy undertaking. That's why the brain subconsciously whispers to itself: Procrastinate, procrastinate! It senses that there's big work ahead. Developing a symphony from a melody or a painting from an image isn't easy. Generating a written plan for a serious business venture is in the same league.

There are several popular misconceptions about the basic purpose of business plans, particularly those describing a brand new venture. Some people promote them as documents for raising money. Others see the plans as essentially legal boilerplate to provide entrepreneurs with "I told you sos" later on if things go sour for outside or inside investors. Still others stress the preparation of a plan as a rite of passage, a cleansing experience that tends to separate the real players from the spectators and camp followers. A perspective that includes all these but is philosophically of much greater use is that *a business plan is a blueprint for building a business.* Few readers would attempt even the addition of a room to their houses without a "picture" from which to work. A business plan is a word picture of what the entrepreneurial dream is, why the dream can be economically viable for those involved, and how the construction will be carried out over time.

As discussed in detail below, a business plan is most usefully thought of as an internal, operating document, not a showpiece for raising money or satisfying attorneys. A sound business plan can be an important contributor to success whenever one, two, three, or more people wish to organize and synchronize a purposeful business effort over time in order to achieve specified results. Whether or not money is raised via the plan, whether or not an attorney ever touches it, whether or not anyone but the writers ever read it, the energy invested in preparing a blueprint most often will have a high rate of return. This is true even, and perhaps especially, when as a result of the effort to put together a workable, believable plan, an idea is abandoned. It's better to cancel a flight at the gate than after takeoff.

Starting a new growth enterprise is normally a relatively high risk proposition. If the venture is successful, that is, economically viable in a projected length of time, everyone is happy, but the challenges of growth are not trivial. If the venture is unsuccessful, careers, money, reputations, spouses, good health, and even lives can be lost. Assuming the leaders of the effort have the necessary personal drive, the height of risk tends to be *inversely* proportional to the presence of two prime ingredients: 1) the directly applicable experience and managing ability of the team responsible for the venture, and 2) the thoroughness of the thinking that goes into the undertaking before it starts. To some extent, they are interchangeable.

Part of the folklore of venture capital is that it is most profitable over the longer haul to bet on good people rather than simply great concepts. "Back a quality individual before backing a surefire idea," was a motto of George Quist of Hambrecht and Quist, one of the oldest and most respected venture capital firms in the country. When pressed to list the indicators of "good people" or "quality individuals," people with proven experience in evaluating entrepreneurs usually include the following:

- Evidence of drive and achievement orientation
- Applicable business or technical experience
- Verifiable integrity
- Ability to communicate ideas and plans

Increasingly, a fifth indicator is finding its way onto the list, namely a propensity toward team work. The turbulent times–current and projected–generate complexity in every aspect of the business world. A variety of skills is needed to cope successfully with the myriad issues that confront any growth company of consequence. No one individual is likely to have all the skills in sufficient depth to do a quality job on a sustained basis. In short, soloists are falling from favor.

A final point of perspective and perhaps clarification is that, by definition, a prospectus is "a report or statement which describes or advertises a forthcoming literary work, a flotation of stock, etc." A prospectus is not a business plan. A business plan, however, may technically be a prospectus if it is used to raise money.

In summary, after preparing a business plan, the entrepreneurial management team should have before it an agreed program–expectations, actions, and results–to which it will willingly commit itself. After reading a business plan, a director, potential investor, or other interested party should know precisely what those involved intend to do, by when, with the human and financial resources called for in the plan.

Preparing a Business Plan

The length and sequence of contents in a business plan for a startup will depend upon the nature of the proposed venture. A major component is almost always needed, however, to describe just why, how, and when economic viability will be accomplished. Other objectives may exist and even seem to be of greater importance to the writers of a given plan, but economic viability is the one necessary condition around which the contents outlined below are molded. Without it, few business ventures, no matter how noble, survive for long. Self-sustaining cash flow, economic viability, is at the heart of being in business.

"Why" is normally addressed by first identifying precisely who outside the enterprise is interested in and qualified to buy whatever it is the enterprise will have to sell, the way it will be sold. "How" is indicated by a complete coverage of the human, production, organizational, and monetary requirements for providing the product or service on a timely and continuing basis consistent with the pricing and quality demands of a chosen marketplace. "When" is reflected by a thorough presentation of the financial implications over time of each important event called for in the plan.

In a plan that is to be read critically by others, it is useful to have an overview or executive summary at the start. Such a section will probably be written last though it appears first. Overall, the contents of a basic blueprint for building a business are as follows:

1.0 CONCEPT

As suggested earlier, there is powerful evidence that the act of committing an idea to paper is a vital step in its development. This is nowhere more true than when dealing with the fundamental idea underlying the formation of a new, growth venture. By nature, new ideas are fuzzy combinations of needs, interests, capabilities, frustration, optimism, ambition, and a dozen other ingredients. Few entrepreneurs wake up one morning with an "aha!" imprinted undeniably on their brains. Instant photography, Internet search engines, fail-safe computers, resoleable tennis shoes, hang gliders, fast food stores, bungee jumping, and microcomputers were not conceived with the help of lightning bolts!

In most instances, a notion or inkling takes some encouragement before it becomes a hunch. A hunch requires some massaging and mulling before it graduates into a discussion piece. A discussion piece demands conversation and research enroute to precarious classification as a full blown idea. An idea takes a lot of work to refine it into a concept upon which to build a business.

With a single, well-developed concept, a massive business empire can be built. But a single product or service is seldom enough to justify the bodily wear and tear required to launch a business intended for the Fortune 500 in the 2000s.

Product/Service	*Possible Concept*
• Quick hamburgers	• Mass-produced restaurant food
• Part-time secretarial help	• Peak load, variable cost labor
• Microcomputer software packages	• Electronic publishing
• Better mouse trap	• Rodent control for home-makers
• Inventory control for small, auto parts retailers	• Hardware/software pack-ages for selected vertical markets
• Solar pool heaters	• Domestic energy transformation devices
• Buggy whips (historic example!)	• Transportation stimulators (!!)
• Raw material control system for paper machines	• Productivity improvements for process industries
• Tennis shoe resoleing	• Apparel recycling

Above are a few examples to illustrate the difference between a product or service and at least one possible underlying concept. The examples do contain a touch of tongue in cheek. It is extremely *unlikely* that all the entrepreneurs responsible for the various products and services shown on the left initially elevated their basic ideas to the conceptual level on the right. The question is whether or not it would have been valuable for them to think the implications of their product or service all the way through to the customer/generic level sooner rather than later (as in Commandment Two).

There is another compelling reason to hammer a concept onto paper in black and white. The possibility of confusion, misunderstanding, and shallowness on the issue of "What business are we in?" is reduced. A rea-

sonably refined concept can help insure that the second
(and third and fourth...) product or service of a budding
enterprise is synergistic and complementary to the first.

CASE H. Engineer Ed came up with a new machine that
sorted bad peanuts from good peanuts on a high-volume
basis. He founded a manufacturing company that did very
well for him and two investors. Based on his initial success,
Ed was able to attract a sizeable amount of investment money
to keep on building the business. He expanded into the distribution of irradiated plastics–a field completely foreign to
his early, peanut machine manufacturing and sales success.
Ed's company peaked out at a modest size.

Make no misunderstanding. Ed did all right for himself financially. But he never built the big company of
his dreams. Ed's eclectic, opportunistic approach has its
place. So does making a big splash with a single product
and then selling the embryonic company to a bigger company interested in expanding its product line. Take the
money and run! Or start over again. It's a matter of what
the founders are out to accomplish (Commandment One).
If you and your associates are out to build a major business, the time invested in identifying and refining your
concept can have a big payoff for you.

2.0 OBJECTIVES

The Third Commandment, covered earlier, stressed
the importance and characteristics of sound objectives.
Two levels of objectives should be included in a business
plan. First, the longer-term interests (intentions, objectives) of the entrepreneur(s) should be identified. Second, the operating objectives–sales, profits, market
share, margins, etc.–need to be spelled out. Both levels
typically require a great deal of digging and iteration.
They need to be in harmony with one another.

On the first level: What do the plan writers hope to achieve for themselves over the longer term? Most everybody, at a minimum, wants to make at least enough money to get along. But there is a huge difference in pursuing $1,000,000 in capital gains within three years and pursuing a steady stream of $75,000 net income per year for life. Neither of these two objectives holds the corner on virtue, but they *are* different. And knowing roughly what you, the plan writer, are after is important. Otherwise, critical readers of the plan don't know what to measure its validity against.

CASE I. Sandra and Kay came up with an idea for a one-stop-shopping phone service for home-repair work. In concept, they envisioned sort of a AAA for commuters who were home owners living in suburbs where people in need of a plumber, electrician, or tree surgeon usually have only the yellow pages for guidance.

The two women spent many hours fleshing out the idea. A thousand questionnaires were mailed to a randomly-selected cross section of the residents in burgeoning Contra Costra County near San Francisco. More than 10 percent of the questionnaires were answered and returned. The answers were encouraging, and the entrepreneurs wisely cross-checked the results with a variety of potential users, suppliers, and community-knowledgeable acquaintances. The end result of the research phase was the finding that the business idea appeared to be capable of supporting one, maybe two, people (owner/managers) modestly.

Is the idea a good one? Should the women proceed? It depends. This is a good example of why it is important for an entrepreneur to know his or her personal objective(s). If Sandra and/or Kay are considering entrepreneuring to get rich, this home-repair idea probably is not the way to do it. If they want to be self-employed while earning a living, it has some possibilities.

Perhaps the biggest mistake to avoid, however, would be for Sandra and Kay to launch into the business with the question of personal objectives unexamined. It's an everyday occurrence to find business partnerships and young corporations on the rocks because the participants found out too late that one of them wanted to reinvest earnings and expand the business while the other preferred to take his or her share of the profits and spend it on long vacations in Europe! Proceeding with a new enterprise made up of people who have mixed motives is what keeps attorneys in BMWs.

Why are *you* interested in building a company? Personal objectives come in many shapes and sizes. Below are seven common measures along which potential starters of businesses might usefully calibrate themselves. Circle a number that corresponds to your personal level of motivation on each measure. Ten is high.

I wish to...

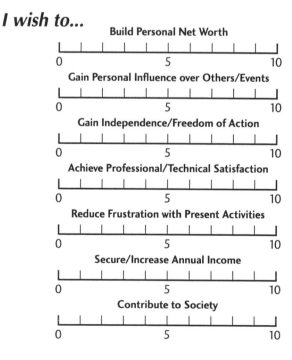

Build Personal Net Worth

0   5   10

Gain Personal Influence over Others/Events

0   5   10

Gain Independence/Freedom of Action

0   5   10

Achieve Professional/Technical Satisfaction

0   5   10

Reduce Frustration with Present Activities

0   5   10

Secure/Increase Annual Income

0   5   10

Contribute to Society

0   5   10

These seven measures are not meant to be the final word. A high number of points on a measure is not necessarily good. There have been hundreds of studies of whether successful entrepreneurs are born or made, renegades from society or heroes, lucky or inspired, identifiable in advance or random marriages of chance and capability. There's a small school of thought in favor of each argument, and chances are good that there will be even more theories in the days ahead as technological advances put immense capabilities at the fingertips of those who are opportunity-minded. When used as points of departure, however, the seven measures above can help an entrepreneur be honest with himself or herself and with the other contributors to the business plan— the blueprint for building the business. One thing is for certain. A business plan written by people with widely-differing or conflicting personal objectives is likely to end up looking more like a camel than the thoroughbred needed to win in a competitive industry.

The second and more obvious level of objectives that should be included in the business plan are those having to do with operating matters such as sales, profits, market share, and so on. The word objective implies *what we are going to make happen*. An objective is more than a wish. It is an *end result* to which resources—cash and people—will be allocated to produce. On the following page are some objectives lifted from a variety of business plans.

- $100,000,000 in sales by fiscal year 2000.
- Market share of 3 percent by end of third year.
- Ninety systems installed and working by 2002.
- Four thousand billable hours by the 24th month.
- Positive cash flow by end of first fiscal year.
- Shipments of 25,000 units within ten months.
- Gross margins increased to 40 percent by tenth quarter.
- Return on Equity of 35 percent per year by third year.
- Positive cash flow of $225,000 in months six through nine.

In short, objectives define the construction checkpoints of the business you are planning to build. Some operating objectives will change from year to year, of course, as various checkpoints are passed and new subjects rise in importance. As objectives change so must the supporting business plan change. The Fourth Commandment is always with you! Prepare and work from a written plan...year after year after year.

There are two trends occurring in the nature of operating objectives as the 1990s skip by. One is that there is an increasing interest across the land in such measures as ROI (Return on Investment) and ROE (Return on Equity). In these times, it is less and less adequate to state merely how you are doing or how you expect to do in a *profit* and *loss* sense. Nowadays the question is more and more: How well do you expect to do with the resources or assets at your disposal? This is more of a *balance sheet* orientation.

For example, on the next page which company is doing better, X or Y?

	Company X	**Company Y**
Sales Last Year	$20,000,000	$30,000,000
Sales Growth over Previous Year	50%	20%
Profit percentage on Sales	15%	5%
Market Position	Strong	Strong

Would your answer be the same if you knew that the total assets (debt and equity) in company X were $10,000,000 and the total assets in company Y were $5,000,000?

Would your answer be different again if you knew that the equity in X was $3,000,000; in Y, $1,000,000? Think about it.

Obviously, your answers—based on the data given—depend on your criteria. Entrepreneurs are increasingly being confronted with the issue of the "quality" of the growth they are projecting. Quality typically is based on a comparison. Upon what asset or equity base is the projected growth—sales and earnings—constructed? Asset *productivity* is another way to think about the challenge facing modern-day managers who must deal with fluctuating interest rates, political gyrations, technological obsolescence, and certain kinds of employee shortages as they build their businesses. The use of objectives (measurable end results to be achieved) has become increasingly important as one of the few antidotes to complexity and confusion in these turbulent times.

Henry David Thoreau once said, "In the long run, men hit only what they aim at." A business plan needs to be aimed at something that is responsive to both the plan writers' personal interests and the known, basic requirements for business success in a chosen marketplace.

3.0 MARKET ANALYSIS

There is a difference between a need and a market. To use a classic example, the management of Ford Motor Company at one point in time perceived a need for a large, flashy car with a lot of gadgetry for the driver. Ford gave the world the Edsel automobile. For a variety of reasons, the perceived need did not turn out to be a market of consequence when the car was introduced. While many people liked the gadgetry, there were only a few people favorably disposed toward buying a large, flashy, futuristic car.

Here is another example. For some years now a few manufacturers have been cultivating, even titillating a need for CD-ROM players in the home. The same is going on today with Internet devices. The cultivating is slowly paying off, and gradually the potential need is being converted around the edges into a market, i.e., a definable group of people favorably disposed toward buying the product. The purpose of the *market* analysis section of a business plan is to identify as precisely as possible the size, location, and characteristics of the set of people who are expected to be favorably disposed toward buying what the new enterprise expects to sell.

Please note with care the contents of the last sentence. It includes: people . . . favorably disposed toward buying. If you are planning to get money in the form of sales dollars from people not yet favorably disposed toward your new product or service, then it is important that you state as much in your market analysis. There's nothing categorically wrong with undertaking to *create* a market. Many entrepreneurs have done it. Doing so requires what is appropriately called missionary marketing. But it's expensive, and your capitalization will have to be sufficient to cover it.

CASE J. The OPEC oil price boost a few years back spawned a number of solar products companies. One of the more exciting ones had a swimming pool heating system based on some technologically-advanced collector panels. The *need* for saving pool heating dollars via solar energy seemed obvious enough. The founder had to decide if there was a market. If so, could that market be reached cost-effectively? Extensive field work indicated that there was a market for solar pool heaters that were within a certain price range. But, having identified a market, it turned out that there was no straightforward way to sell to and service it. The founder faced the hard choice of abandoning his idea or assembling a distribution system from scratch. He raised enough money to do the latter.

Once isolated, the total population of all potential buyers (consumers or corporate representatives such as purchasing agents, officers, or department heads) for a given product or service is a certain size. Call it X. Within X there are discrete subgroups called segments that vary in characteristics such as the reason for buying, financial ability to pay, and ease of reaching. Most entrepreneurs need to select a segment or a very limited number of segments upon which to concentrate available selling efforts. In this Market Analysis section of your business plan, you are interested primarily in describing the magnitude and nature of the business opportunity, usually in terms of segments. Later sections in the plan deal with how you expect to pursue the opportunity in the chosen segment(s).

What are the characteristics of markets that are attractive bets to growth company investors? A rough outline of the criteria used by a cross section of west coast venture capitalists follows.

The targeted market should be:

- Over $50,000,000 in total size (annual sales volume).
- Growing at a rate significantly greater than the real GNP.
- Sufficiently fragmented or noncompetitive to allow an aggressive new entry to grow to $25,000,000 or more in sales within five years.
- Amenable to profit making by a new entry at a rate of at least 5 to 10 percent (after tax) on sales within two to three years after startup.
- Socially and politically acceptable to the business world in general so that:
  a. Traditional forms of financing such as bank loans are available to the company once it is established.
  b. Sale of stock to the public or a larger corporation at a fair price is possible at some point in time.

This outline is, as stated, rough. There is a lot of art in making venture investments. Often the precise size of a market is not quantifiable. How big is the Internet market, for example? How big will it be in 2000? However, if a market is currently $10,000,000 in size and it is predicted to grow at 50 percent a year for ten years, there may be plenty of room for a new entry! The overriding issue is whether there appear to be enough available, profitable sales dollars to support the proposed new enterprise over a reasonable length of time so that it can develop a track record as a growth company.

One other point of great importance bears repeating. There are many good and proper reasons for entrepreneuring. Running a company up in size and selling out for a healthy capital gain is only one of them.

But whatever the reason, an appropriate market must exist or be developed to satisfy the top-line requirements dictated by the objectives of the primary participants. If there are inadequate sales, the top line, there will be anemic profits, if any, which is the bottom line. More on this in Commandment Seven.

Once the plan writers have developed a comprehensive picture of the market to be pursued, the supporting or amplifying elements are relatively straightforward:

- What or who are any intermediate influences on the ultimate buyers? For example, will you have to work through dealers, distributors, TV producers, sales representatives, associations, purchasing agents, or retailers? What hurdles or opportunities do they present?
- What are the existing and anticipated competitive conditions? How will they affect pricing, hiring, packaging, facility location, and transportation?
- Are there important governmental influences in the chosen market, such as those affecting the five E's: energy, equality, ethics, environment, and employment practices?

Where does one obtain market data? The list of sources is infinitely long. Appendix A contains a handy note used at the Harvard Business School that suggests some of the prime possibilities for developing a picture of an industry or market opportunity. Ideally, one or more members on the entrepreneuring team has in-depth experience in the market to begin with. If not, triple the importance of this section of your plan!

In summary, no one should try harder to understand the dynamics of the targeted marketplace than the aspiring entrepreneur, the potential new kid on the block. Ultimately, business success flows from satisfying customers (Commandment Two).

4.0 PRODUCTION

There are a variety of ways to make most products. The mix between capital equipment and labor, made parts and bought parts, assemble here versus assemble there, and so forth, has to be worked out. Every decision has implications for product delivery times, cash flow, quality control requirements, and other elements of a manufacturing business such as staffing and facility requirements. Likewise, service business management teams face early choices which often set a new business on a path from which it may be quite hard to turn later. Location is a major consideration if customers need direct access to the business. People, high skill or low, must be available nearby or via their electronic connections. It is hard to produce custom wood furniture without skilled woodworkers, for example. In summary, given a positive point of view about an identified market opportunity, production to capitalize on that opportunity is a key blueprint ingredient.

Production plans probably flow easiest from hard to soft, that is, from equipment lists to systems considerations and people, once a production philosophy has been established. Production philosophies generally start with a decision about where the company will position itself on the make-versus-buy continuum. There are two well-known, high-flying, publicly-held computer companies that have each exceeded $100,000,000 in sales in recent years. Neither actually manufactures more than about 15 percent of its own hardware. Eighty-five percent of every system they ship consists of vendor-supplied parts. This ratio is neither good nor bad, only different from the more traditional pattern of making what you sell. The ratio merely reflects what two different management teams have decided is best for their own enterprises.

What is best for your particular enterprise? There is no clean answer. It depends most on what it is your management team does best and where the money tends to get spent in your chosen industry. Take a look at the example below. A and B are cost distribution averages from two completely different industries and marketplaces. The management of a new company entering either industry should know the relevant averages.

Industry A Averages		Industry B Averages
.08	Transportation	.15
.35	Distributors	.00
.00	Sales Representative	.10
.15	Internal Sales Force & Marketing	.10
.20	Cost of Goods Sold	.45
.22	Overhead, R&D, Profit	.20
$1.00	One Sales Dollar	$1.00

On average, more than half ($.58) of industry A's dollars of revenue go to moving the product after it is in inventory. Only $.20 is spent on cost of goods sold. On average, on the other hand, companies in industry B spend $.45 on the cost of goods sold. So there is at least a preliminary argument that says a new company entering industry A might wish to allocate the bulk of its primary resources to excelling in non-manufacturing matters if it is possible to do so. An entrepreneur who can beat the $.58 average may have a distinct, competitive advantage. A new company tackling industry B, in contrast, may wish to consider a production philosophy that leans more toward excelling in manufacturing, assembly, or fabrication. If the industry B entrepreneur can beat the $.45 average, he or she may have a competitive advantage.

CASE K. In 1993 three men formed a new company with $250,000 of outside capital and a concept fashioned around user-friendly inventory control systems for selected vertical markets. The company, which was selling a $30,000 item to small proprietorships which typically had annual sales of under $1,000,000, was operating in the black after its second quarter in existence. It has been immensely profitable every quarter since, and today it enjoys sales exceeding $100,000,000 a year. It has also gone public and maintained a high price/earnings ratio for some time now.

From its inception, the management in Case K minimized the amount of manufacturing done in-house. Essentially all parts were purchased. Assembly work was even subcontracted to a variety of suppliers. "I didn't want for us to have to build big parking lots on expensive real estate," said the president in an interview." Only the quality control part of production is done in-house. We have built our own staff in other areas where we think we are experts–marketing, sales, and engineering. We're happy to let others [vendors] make a buck. They can take the ebb and flow of hiring and laying off production people. They can own the parking lots!"

CASE L. A new bank was formed in a medium-sized metropolitan city with a population of 100,000. It was to be the only independent bank in the area. The founders were able to attract a sizeable block of opening capital. How should that capital be allocated (beyond buying a vault!)? A fancy building and offices? Staff? Computers and systems? Automated tellers? Marketing? Product development?

Some money had to go to each category, of course, but a carefully reasoned decision was made to put the lion's share into the staff rather than into buildings, marketing, or high speed production and processing systems, where no matter how much was spent, the new bank could not excel against competition. The founders did, however, go out and hire the premier people (from other banks, naturally) in the area. The new bank exceeded its second year projections fifteen months after opening its modest doors for business.

What worked in Cases K and L are not formulas for you. The cases merely illustrate the point that a production philosophy needs to be thought through carefully before plans are made to spend money on real state, bricks, mortar, people, or equipment. Peter Drucker points out in his book, *Managing In Turbulent Times,* that we are rapidly becoming a nation of knowledge workers. One manifestation of that trend is a change in the historic mix in how scarce resources are allocated between sales, production, marketing, managing, and R&D activities.

Back to the business plan itself. Given a basic production philosophy, what then? It's time to get down to details:

- What processes are involved and how will they be obtained?
- What equipment is needed to support or provoke efficient, in-house operations?
- Given the above, what are the facility requirements?
- What is to be the source of raw materials, labor, supplies, and purchased parts? Who will oversee sourcing in the company?
- How will incoming inspection, quality control, packaging, transportation, and repairs be managed?
- What is the schedule of who is to do what, by when, regarding production?
- From the above, what is the budget, i.e., the timing and magnitude of expenditures?
- What will be done if the business grows much faster than expected? Or much, much slower?

As a general rule, the leaner a young enterprise is, the better. Money tied up in facilities, inventories, equipment, and other fixed costs reduces the ability of management to maneuver and adjust its plans and actions to changing conditions. At the same time, sufficient control over the production of the customer satisfaction–product or service–to be sold is important. The best marketing program in the world will be wasted if the demand generated goes unsatisfied due to quality, cost, or delivery problems. Smart, disciplined decisions about the allocation of scarce resources are one mark of people who can excel in entrepreneuring.

5.0 MARKETING

As used here, marketing is a broad term that includes all aspects of creating and keeping customers. A business plan should reflect a detailed description of precisely how the targeted population described in the market analysis (section 3.0) will be allowed or coaxed to exchange its change for your product and/or service on a continuing basis. Here are some of the questions to be answered:

- How will customers' needs be identified, classified, and fed into the workings of the business?
- How will customer satisfaction be tracked?
- What methods of selling and advertising and communicating are to be used to carry the messages of your business to the intended audiences?
- What will make the chosen channels of distribution productive, e.g., incentive systems, packaging innovations?
- What product or service features and benefits are to be emphasized? How do they stack up against competition?
- How are credit approval, collections, and complaints to be administered?
- Who is involved in pricing decisions, and what is the basis for decisions, e.g., cost, value added, value to customer?

- What are the plans for the development and/or evolution of the product or service?
- What level, if any, of research activities are needed to sustain or accelerate the growth of business?
  [Note: Technology can be a separate and very large section of a total business plan, particularly for a technology-based venture. In such a section, the management team needs to spell out who or what will drive the needed development effort as well as what is expected to be accomplished, by when.]
- What responses by competitors are likely, if any, and how will they be countered, if at all?
- What is the schedule of who is to do what, by when, regarding marketing?
- From the above, what is the budget, the timing, and the magnitude of expenditures?
- What will be done if the business grows much faster than expected? Much, much slower than expected?

There is always an element of guesswork in predicting what is going to happen in the marketplace. This is one powerful reason why the width of management's experience base in the chosen industry is of major importance to an outsider evaluating a proposed business. The broader the base, the more valid management's expectations should be and the less likelihood there is of surprises. Candidates for entrepreneuring who have backgrounds in the steel industry are going to be less than convincing when they describe their campaign to dominate the world yogurt market.

Here is a final point of perspective under the general heading of marketing. You may have noted that the word strategy has not been used so far in this material on Preparing a Business Plan. It is a word that has been overpublicized to the point of confusion. Everything is a strategy. As a practical matter, there are potentially three levels of strategy in a growth company: Corporate,

Business, and Functional. **Corporate strategy** has to do with what business or businesses the enterprise will be in...and by exclusion, therefore, not in. Then, hopefully, each of the one or more businesses in a given corporation has a discrete **business strategy.** This is best defined as a summary statement covering what will be sold, to whom, in pursuit of the expectations that have been set for the business unit. And finally, within a given business unit, there are usually **functional strategies** for manufacturing, marketing, finance, purchasing, personnel, and so on, that summarize how objectives will be pursued.

In the marketing section of a business plan, all three levels of strategy may well be covered, but typically the emphasis is on business and functional issues. In a single business company—such as most new companies—the corporate and business strategies are one and the same anyway. Fundamentally, there are only six basic *business* strategies: product line expansion, market expansion, forward integration, backward integration, diversification, and, of course, home base, i.e., continuing to sell just what you have been to your existing customers.

Basic Business Strategies for Building a Business

Once again, a statement of *business* strategy boils down to: What is to be sold, to whom. This brings us back full circle to the job of marketing. Marketing is the primary interface between an enterprise and the outside, operating environment. Young growth companies usually need smart marketing even if they do have a better mousetrap of some kind.

6.0 ORGANIZATION AND PEOPLE

People make things happen. The right people make the right things happen. Selecting and fitting the right people to key responsibilities is a continuous process that ideally starts before or at the time the business plan is developed so that the document truly reflects the input of the team that is to execute it. There are at least four layers of talent potentially active in an enterprise: a board of directors or advisors, the general management, functional specialists, and other key individuals. Some people will contribute in more than one role.

As suggested in Commandment One, directors are often chosen for convenience rather than for the specific talents they might bring to the organization. This is a mistake. Qualified, interested, informed directors can be useful in guiding a company to economic viability and beyond. Properly used, a board can be an internal consulting group or a sounding board for management rather than just a legal appendage or a comfortable formality for the chief executive officer. The top layer of talent, the board of directors or advisors, should provide perspective based on solid, related experience.

As indicated earlier in this Fourth Commandment, quality managing is a prime ingredient for success in most growth companies. Managing here is defined as setting expectations and achieving results through (not with or for) others. Almost every outstanding team in any field of endeavor has one or more good coaches, people responsible for the results who must pursue those results via their subordinates or associates. In smaller companies, most of the key people often have to wear a manager's (coach's) hat part of the time and a doer's hat the rest of the time. Under such circumstances, it's easy for the distinction between the two different kinds of work to become blurred. *Both kinds of work are necessary for successful entrepreneuring.*

When blurring occurs, it is often the managing work that gets shoved aside in the rush of day-to-day pressures to obtain orders, finish designs, produce goods, and ship things. A proper organization design will insure that managers are in place and motivated and free to spend the necessary time on planning and supervising others in pursuit of the expectations of the enterprise, i.e., the vision, mission, and objectives.

CASE M. During the tennis boom of the mid-1970s, a number of the major tennis stars of that era started tennis-related businesses. One such business grew to several million dollars in sales from a diverse set of activities that included publishing, player management, tennis training camps, retail stores, and tournament promotion. The star-studded company lost money hand over fist. To reverse the loss, a CPA was hired to fix the company. She installed the necessary control systems and generally helped the company back to the point where it was at least breaking even.

After successfully completing this turn-around task, she was made president. But no other managers or supervisors, e.g., to oversee the accounting function, were added to pick up that layer of the rather complex operations. The CPA simply had two big jobs now instead of one: she was both the general manager and the accounting & control manager. Within a year the company was deep in the red again, and the president was both burned out and fired.

What is the moral of the story? Just below the director or advisor layer of talent, there is a layer of general management that must be provided for in the organization design of a new venture if the founders and/or investors wish to avoid having an *adventure* on their hands. Most everyone who has been successful at doing something (selling, engineering, programming, accounting, etc.) assumes he or she can also manage. *This is a faulty assumption.* More on this later in Commandment Five. Sound management is the second required layer of talent.

As a general rule, among the members of the management team and the board, the primary functional skills–sales & marketing, production, accounting, finance, personnel, and technology (if appropriate)– should be well represented. Functional skills are the third layer of talent. It is not a problem if some functional skills are provided initially by board members–or possibly by consultants or part-timers–rather than by full-time members of the company. This condition can be altered in time as the business grows. The important point for the entrepreneur is that he or she should not try to fly on one wing during the critical early days when there is a natural tendency to try to do everything oneself. If you want to build a growth company, get the money you need to get the people you need to do what the business must have done well to succeed in an unforgiving, competitive environment. If you can't get the money you need, consider dropping or radically altering your concept. Retreat? Hell no! You merely back up to go around and try it another way.

The fourth layer of talent in most embryonic organizations is the one that contains the one or two or more key individuals who possess the special talents indigenous to the specific business. A semiconductor company must have a solid-state physicist. A software company must have a senior programmer. A new bank probably needs at least one banker. Case M above was critically dependent upon tennis camp directors who could both play and manage. And a chocolate chip cookie company that started in Palo Alto, CA. clearly needed a skilled baker with high volume production experience. Sometimes the president or another officer is also the key, special talent. This works all right so long as the individual can keep his or her multiple jobs separate and well covered—either directly or via delegation.

Functional Structure

What about structure, i.e., organization design? Most new growth enterprises begin with a functional structure which contains one level of general management, a president, with functional vice-presidents filling out the team. There are other possibilities, of course. The vice-presidents could be responsible for products or geographic areas, for example, instead of functions, but usually such "profit center" designs with their multiple layers of general management make more sense later on. For a new company intent on growth, a simple functional organization with simple titles, if any, and an articulated policy of organizational flexibility over time is probably the best approach. In the business plan, then, the writer or writers identify the starting point. The purpose of the initial design is to support the business strategy of the enterprise. In most cases, the design should be purposefully changed over time as the enterprise changes in size and complexity.

Given a structural starting point, here are the major supporting details that can usefully be included under organization in a business plan:

- Who is accountable to whom, and for what?
- What pay, incentives, benefits, and promotion sequences will be used to attract, stimulate, and hold on to desired people?
- How will salaries be determined and administered over time?
- When and where will various people be added to the organization over, say, the first year or so?
- From the above, what is the budget, the timing, and the magnitude of expenditures?

Capable people who understand what they are to accomplish and who are motivated to invest their energies in the enterprise are the basic building blocks of entrepreneuring. Increasing attention is being paid today to the people side of business. "Our perspective is that organizations are organic, not mechanical or hydraulic," say authors Pascale and Athos in their frame-breaking book, *The Art of Japanese Management.* The development of a positive, energetic, corporate culture is best begun when an organization is small. The amount of thought put into the organization design is frequently a useful, early indicator of the amount of attention that will be paid to the people factors in the equation for success, however defined.

7.0 FUNDS FLOW AND FINANCIAL PROJECTIONS

Startup money (initial capitalization) is the temporary glue that holds the building blocks of a new company together until the merit of the company's product or service is widely enough recognized and valued in the marketplace to generate the earnings needed to support and build the business. The amount and timing of the startup money needed is derived primarily from the production, marketing, organizational, and perhaps technology sections of the business plan discussed earlier. Many new companies do not require startup money from outside investors. Some do.

Entrepreneurs often worry about how much of their companies they will have to "give up" to investors before they worry about how much glue they need to successfully launch the enterprise. This is backward thinking. A healthier perspective goes something like this: 1) The needs of the business should dictate the amount and timing of the capital required. It probably takes less to start a consulting practice than it does to found a toy company. 2) If the amount required exceeds what the founder(s) can provide, he, she or they should consider raising the incremental money needed from investors. It is usually better to bring in outside money than to start short, i.e., thinly capitalized. And it is often easier to raise money before starting operations than to try to do so after starting when cash gets tight. 3) For those with growth-company ambitions, it is better to own a small piece of a big pie than vice versa. Money is a continuing need in a growth company. The aspiring entrepreneur who is unable to appreciate (and/or raise) other people's money may be better off setting more modest expectations for himself or herself. 4) Recognize that you are not giving up anything when you bring in outside money, you are *selling* a piece of the company. 5) If you decide to use them, solicit buyers (investors) who are in synch with your objectives. Be well prepared to negotiate the price.

The amount of money you are able to get for a portion of your company will depend on:

- How much money is needed.
- The magnitude and shape (rewards/risks) of the opportunity.
- The background of the management team.
- The quality of the business plan.
- The chemistry between the individuals involved.
- What's going on in the world at the time of the decision.

It's academic to worry about "giving up an arm and a leg" until you have crystallized the size of the transaction. A detailed, realistic cash flow projection is the basic technique for determining the needs of a growth business.

A cash flow projection consists of three fundamental elements: cash in, cash out, and timing. A skeleton projection is shown on the top of the next page.

Look first at the bottom item, q, labeled Cumulative Cash Position. This is the primary line to heed. An enterprise cannot operate long with zero cash, and it certainly can't grow. In many respects, a complete Cash Flow Projection is a quantitative summary of how you and your associates intend to build the enterprise. Item q is your fuel gauge. [One side comment: Today there are excellent cash flow projection software programs available. By using such a program, prospective entrepreneurs can play "what if" with their cash flow planning without resorting to endless hours with pencils, erasers, and accounting paper.]

The periods at the top of the projection can be months, quarters, or years. Typically, a business plan for a substantial enterprise will show months for the first year or two, quarters for an additional year or two, and years for the balance up to a total of four or five years. While few readers expect the later years' projections to turn

Outline: Cash Flow Projection

Periods		1	2	3 . .TOTALS
Dates		Jan.	Feb.	Mar.
Cash In				
a.	Units Sold			
b.	Units Shipped/Provided			
c.	Price/Unit			
d.	$ of Net Sales			
e.	Sales $ Rec'd			
f.	Discounts, Commissions Paid			
g.	Net Cash In			
Cash Out				
h.	Cost of Goods Sold			
	1. Purchases			
	2. Materials			
	3. Labor			
i.	Management			
j.	Marketing			
k.	Administration			
l.	Rent, Utilities, Phone			
m.	Net Cash Out			
n.	Cash Flow/Period			
o.	Starting Cash			
p.	Net Cash Flow			
q.	Cumulative Cash Position			

out to be 100 percent accurate, it is important that growth company managers think through their opportunity beyond a year or so, even if there are major unknowns.

Items a and b, Units Sold and Units Shipped/Provided, are increasingly important indicators of the reasonableness of a given plan. The units can be units of service, contracts, boxes of product, gallons–whatever is the basic element of transaction in the business. If the rate at which units move is suspect, the validity of the entire cash flow will be open to question.

Picture this. Four people conceive an idea for a new company and prepare the following as part of their cash flow projection. How would you evaluate the figures shown?

	Year 1	Year 2	Year 3
Units Sold	1000	2,300,000	9,000,000
Units Shipped	1000	2,000,000	8,000,000

	Yes	No
a. *Looks like an exciting growth opportunity.*	___	___
b. *The year-to-year increases are quite sizeable, particularly between year one and year two.*	___	___
c. *The management will need to know a lot about marketing and production.*	___	___

Of course it's hard to make a determination without knowing what makes up the units. If the units were toothpicks, one conclusion might be reached. If the units are aluminum wheelbarrows, another conclusion! Regardless of the units, however, choice b is true, and probably so is choice c. Any management that is going to increase output by 2000 times over a twenty-four month period (Year 1-2) has its work cut out for it. Optimism is important in entrepreneuring, alongside realism.

Returning to the Outline: Cash Flow Projection, items c through m are straightforward. For a complicated business, e.g., one with a lot of engineering or high science, the number of line items included in the cash in and cash out calculations might number 100 or more. The important thing is to identify all the significant cash sources and uses. Doing so will reduce, but not eliminate, the downstream surprises.

Item n is item g minus item m. This Cash Flow/Period is the *actual* cash in hand at the end of the particular month, quarter, or year. [Note: the difference between items d and e is that d is the figure for invoices mailed;

OPERATING STATEMENT

	19XX	19XY	19XZ
Sales			
Cost of Sales			
Gross Margin			
Marketing			
Management			
Engineering			
Administration			
Other			
Operating Profit			
Taxes			
Net Profit			

BALANCE SHEET

	19XX	19XY	19XZ
Assets			
Cash			
Inventory			
Accounts Receivable			
Buildings, Equipment			
Total Assets			
Liabilities			
Accounts Payable			
Loans			
Net Worth			
Capital Invested			
Earnings Retained			
Total Liabilities & Net Worth			

e is the cash actually received from customers. If your customers take sixty days to pay you, there is a sixty-day lag between sales and receipts.]

Item o, Starting Cash, can be *the* plug figure for a new enterprise, that is, the amount of capital required to keep item q, Cumulative Cash Flow, positive. Try doing your early projections with zero Starting Cash in order to determine how deep the worst-case hole is and when it occurs. By approaching the projections in this way, you and your associates force onto paper the nitty-gritty dynamics of the business—what it takes to pay the bills! If you *can't do* a cash flow projection with confidence, you don't understand your business. If you *won't do* a serious cash flow projection that others can critically review, you are kidding yourself about wanting to succeed in big-league entrepreneuring.

From the cash flow projections come the other two major financial indicators you will need: projected operating statements (profit and loss) and projected balance sheets. A skeleton Operating Statement and a skeleton Balance Sheet are included on the previous page for your review.

An Operating Statement summarizes what happened in terms of revenues and expenses during a specified *period of time*. A Balance Sheet is a snapshot of the total financial circumstances of an enterprise—any enterprise from a church to General Motors—at a specified *point in time*. At any such point in time, the sum of the assets must add up to the sum of the liabilities plus the net worth of the enterprise.

There are literally dozens of fine, readable textbooks which include information on how to develop financial statements such as the three described briefly above. Therefore, the details of doing so have not been included in this material on Preparing a Business Plan. Suffice it to say that one or more people on an emerging company's management team must be at home with the financial and accounting elements of the business.

The funds flow and financial projections section of the business plan summarizes all of the previous sections in terms of dollars coming and going. At a minimum, this section will include the following projections covering a period of typically two to five years from the time of the business plan:

> Projected Cash Flow Projection
> Projected Operating Statements
> Projected Balance Sheets

With this information, reasoned "guesstimates" about the future value of the company can be made. In addition, the magnitude and timing of money needs should be roughly evident. Now, questions of the appropriate legal form of the business—sole proprietorship, partnership, corporation, etc.—as well as the nature of any deal with outside investors can be productively addressed.

8.0 OWNERSHIP

Once the requirements of the business are identified via a thoughtful planning process, the question of ownership form and percentages can be tackled.

While all ventures benefit from a business plan, many ventures do not require outside money. For those that do, it is probably obvious that a highly experienced, two-person founding team of an enterprise in need of $2 million in capital faces a somewhat different situation than a young, five-person team in need of only $200,000. That's why general rules for deal making are of limited value. They never fit the particular circumstance. The overriding principle is quite simple, however: All the primary participants should feel that any deal finally agreed to is essentially fair. Smart outside investors don't want to put money into a company which has some unhappy team members because they feel they were "done wrong."

And smart entrepreneurs don't want unhappy investors who walk away or send in their lawyers the next time money is required or the first time the company bumps into a crisis.

The relative merits of regular corporations versus Subchapter S corporations versus partnerships will not be covered here. There are a number of sources of advice on the subject. Your primary guidance should come from your chosen legal and accounting help (see Commandment One). Likewise, the merits of common stock versus convertible preferred stock versus various debt instruments are beyond the scope of this commandment. What this ownership section of your business plan should show is your conclusions on these matters plus a recommended financing and ownership scheme covering the time period used in the financial projections.

What should the ownership split be in a startup? Consider a relatively simple case first. Suppose $1 million is needed for a new venture and it has two founders who will personally invest $250,000 each to provide half the total amount needed. In this case, it is clear that the two founders will sell no more than 50 percent of the business to raise the remaining $500,000. If they have a lot of germane experience and have worked long and hard to develop a plan and line up people, it's likely that they have a strong argument for retaining more than 50 percent of the company for their $500,000 investment. They are putting their money on the line, as well as their careers. If their proposed venture excites prospective investors, it is possible the entrepreneurs in this case can raise the missing $500,000 they need by selling somewhere between 20 and 40 percent of the company...thereby keeping 60 to 80 percent. [Note: In this case, they also *might* be able to borrow part or all of the missing $500,000 and, thereby, further reduce the need for outside equity money.]

Consider a more complex case. Suppose, once again, that $1 million is needed for a new venture. But this time assume there are four prospective founders, two of whom have key technical ideas and expertise and two of whom have broad, relevant business experience. None of the four is able to invest any part of $1 million, but all four will have to leave high-paying jobs to join the new enterprise team where their salaries will be somewhat less. What's fair in this instance? Chances are that the founding team in total may end up with 10 to 40 percent of the company *over time* via stock options, staged financing, and other agreed upon mechanisms. This percentage assumes the founders are dealing with professional investors and advisors. It might be possible for the founders to achieve a higher percentage if they are willing to sell part of their enterprise to people who are not professional investors. But this alternative has drawbacks that must be considered by the founders of a potential growth business. For example, if more investment money is needed later, such subsequent rounds of financing (from professional money sources) may be quite difficult if the company's ownership is already spread around somewhat indiscriminately. It is always a challenge to figure out ways to attract and compensate key, noncash contributors who will go onto the payroll of a startup operation. A competent, interested legal firm with rounded new-enterprise experience will have seen many combinations and permutations. You don't need to reinvent the wheel.

What if no outside money is needed at all? Suppose two, three, or more people happen onto an opportunity and they can finance the startup themselves. In this third case, any ownership split is pretty much a matter of negotiation between the parties with this proviso: At the earliest possible moment after the business plan is formulated, all the parties involved in the ownership should agree upon and sign a written buy/sell agreement that spells out precisely what procedures will be followed in the event that one or more of the parties wishes or is forced to disengage from the enterprise. The time to hammer out such an agreement with the help of an experienced attorney is before the company gets going. Do it *now*. Tomorrow is frequently too late.

The ownership section of a business plan should cover the entrepreneur's program for financing the business over time including:

- The legal form of the enterprise.
- The nature of the initial financing envisioned, including pricing and the resulting ownership distribution.
- The nature of projected future rounds of financing, including planned pricing and the resulting ownership distribution.
- The projected returns that any investors will enjoy on the money they have invested in the enterprise.

This last element of information, the projected returns, can often serve handily as the centerpiece of an Overview that you, the writer, prepares and includes at the very front of your business plan.

In summary, this, the Fourth Commandment, stresses the importance of developing a written plan. Such a plan may turn out to be nothing more than an exercise. Done properly, a plan is really a blueprint of the proposed undertaking, done in advance, using the best available information and judgment. The blueprint is a representation, not the business itself. It is a dry run, a simulation. The results of the planning effort may turn out to be negative, i.e., the idea won't work, even on paper! Or, when thoughtfully calculated, the risk/reward ratio may be quite high, too high to attract capital and people. More likely than not, the very effort required to sweat through the development of a comprehensive plan will dissuade many potential entrepreneurs. This is as it should be, and by turning back early they will possibly save themselves from the pain of failing. Business building in these times is not a sure thing. Entrepreneuring isn't for the faint of heart. "Far better it is to dare mighty things . . .," said Teddy Roosevelt. Getting the "things" down on paper is a useful filtering process before you dare.

Appendix B contains a Guide to Preparing a Business Plan including a table of contents.

EXERCISE

Appendix C contains a complete business plan for a new enterprise, the Cdex Corporation—an early, microcomputer software company. It is an actual plan that was reviewed by a number of venture capitalists. Read and evaluate it. What, in your opinion, are its strengths and weaknesses? Note them on the page provided. Then look over the venture capitalists' comments that follow in the Epilogue.

Hiring Smart

THE FIFTH COMMANDMENT

EMPLOY KEY PEOPLE WITH PROVEN RECORDS OF SUCCESS AT DOING WHAT NEEDS TO BE DONE IN A MANNER CONSISTENT WITH THE DESIRED VALUE SYS- TEM OF THE ENTERPRISE.

People do what they like; they like what they know. Experience adds depth to knowledge. The best indicator of how a person will perform in the future is how he or she has done in the past in the same or related activity. Criteria for selecting key people is dictated by the plan, the blueprint, for the business. A brickmason is not needed to construct a wooden building. The plan reflects the operational objectives, the work-a-day culture, and the intentions of the primary participants. The interests and capabilities of a new key person must harmonize with all three.

Commandment One dealt with the primary participants–directors, advisors, officers, and unique employees. Commandment Five has to do with setting the stage
for the expanding and ultimately much larger group of
people upon whom a growth company sooner or later
must depend.

There are two sides to the key-people coin. One side
has to do with qualifications in a technical or functional
sense; the other has to do with what can best be termed
attitude, or, in somewhat fancier terms, proclivity to pitch
in and enthusiastically participate in building the enterprise. The proper selection of exactly the right key
people is akin to building sturdy, square corners on a
house under construction which greatly simplifies the
later addition of roof joists, wallboard, and siding. Sound,
early decisions in picking lead salespeople, supervisors,
and senior technicians, greatly simplifies decision making and cooperation as the enterprise grows.

CASE N. Ralph X's itch to run his own show became un-
bearable, and he looked long and hard for an opportunity
he could get his arms around. After a number of months he
found something that really excited his imagination. He
found it literally right in his own backyard. Ralph was an
avid small boat sailor, and he was at the time the champion
in his class of high performance, two-person boats, a prominent class in the area. One Saturday after racing Ralph heard
that the manufacturer of his boat was on the brink of bankruptcy, primarily due to mismanagement by the boat's designer (who was also the boat company's owner and president).

Ralph checked into the matter, analyzed the situation
in depth, prepared an extensive business plan, and raised
$200,000 from a group of eight individuals during a period
when most other entrepreneurs were having difficulty in getting money. Ralph left his middle management job, put together a smart board of directors, hired a sales vice-presi

(case continued on next page)

dent with extensive boating industry experience, and prepared to set up boat production. He purchased the fiberglass molds and exclusive rights to the design and name
from the then-defunct boat designer and manufacturer. A
lot of Ralph's time the first few months was spent assuring
dealers across the country that there would be plenty of new,
quality boats to sell by the following spring season. He then
turned to manufacturing. For a variety of reasons, expediency among them, Ralph hired the original boat designer,
call him Y, to head up production. Y picked a plant site on
the nearby coast, hired a crew, lined up suppliers, and started
building boats for Ralph according to the schedules called
for in the business plan.

What outcome would you predict for Case N? To summarize a long, painful story, the promise of the business
plan was never fulfilled. Y produced poor quality, overly
costly boats that were shipped into the distribution/
dealer system. Ralph scrambled to identify and correct
the problems. It turned out that the plant was in a poor
location and the supply of knowledgeable, dependable
labor was erratic at best. By the time Ralph replaced Y
and relocated the plant, the damage to the boats' reputation in the field was severe and a boat selling season
had passed. During the period of troubles, two new competitors with comparable boats entered the picture.
Ralph was never able to regain the original momentum
with which he had started despite his expenditure of a
lot of extra money on advertising to the trade. He bor-
rowed the money to finance the extra advertising, and
he (unwisely, in desperation) personally signed a guarantee for the loan to his company. Five years later Ralph
is still paying off the debt out of the salary he earns
working for a large real estate firm.

Hindsight is always 20/20, of course, but it is clear
that for entrepreneurs there is no substitute for hiring

proven experience in doing what the enterprise needs to have done. In this case, Ralph needed someone who had produced high quality, relatively high priced fiberglass units in volume within tight cost parameters. What he got was a nice guy who loved the boat and had made several thousand of them essentially one at a time.

Entrepreneurs are always under time pressures, very often self-imposed. Expediency sometimes prevails over tight thinking. Nowhere is it as costly to err as in the selection of people around whom essential functional or technical activities will revolve.

How do you protect yourself?

Here are four suggestions:

- Tough face-to-face discussions
- Reference checks
- Scenario questioning
- Multiple interviewers

Tough face-to-face discussions. Entrepreneurs tend to be outgoing and optimistic in nature. It goes with the territory. You like to be liked. Most people do. It's natural to look for the best in people; doing so makes for a smoother world. Most anyone you are going to interview for a key position is going to have at least fairly good oral skills, especially salespeople. You've got to cut through the fuzz and get to the heart of the matter. *What specifically has the person done and accomplished during the last few years?*

Use the interviewee's resume or application as a chronological guide and then ask open questions (Tell me about . . .) to dig out exactly what the candidate has done every month for the past sixty months. Ask for details. Make notes. Clarify discrepancies. Question gaps. Identify accomplishments. When you are done with the interview, you should thoroughly understand the candidate's proven record and his or her feeling about it. If you are not comfortable extracting such details, turn the job over to another primary participant who is.

Reference checks. With sixty months of activity in hand you are well equipped to verify the highlights and gather additional insight into any key person you are considering adding to the team. Phone two or more references and ask them to tell you about the candidate. Seed the conversation with specific questions from your notes in order to refresh memories. In particular, try to pick up extra input on the candidate's attitude–more about this later in this commandment–and personality. You are not necessarily looking for someone who "fits in" in a conforming sense of the words. But in a smaller company the chemistry between individuals is important. There's nowhere to hide. Besides, the more you know about someone, the better you will be able to guide and help him or her succeed in your company.

Scenario questioning. In a second or third meeting with a candidate, pose some "what if" questions. For example, think back to Ralph and his fiberglass boat company. Suppose he had asked Y one or more of the following questions:

-Tell me, Y, what specifically would you do if we found that our production costs per boat were running 25 percent over budget two months in a row?

-Say, Y, how would you respond to a sudden increase in orders–10 or 20 more boats per week than we planned?

-What would you do if a union tried to organize the plant?

-Tell me about your approach to inventory control, Y.

-Outline for me, if you don't mind, how you would go about assuring that we have boats with zero defects shipped to our customers.

Y's answer to the last question would probably have been a humdinger!

Scenario questioning can help you separate those people who really know what they're about and those who are playing it by ear and hoping they can handle whatever arises. It's the difference between proven experience and potential. It's OK to hire potential as long as you know what you are getting and you are willing to fill in for the lack of relevant experience and seasoning in one way or other to get done what needs to be done, in accordance with your business plan.

Multiple interviewers. No matter how bright you are, Ms. or Mr. Entrepreneur, you will still tend to hire in your own image. We all do it. For this reason alone it is useful to get other people's reactions to candidates you are considering for key positions. In addition, it is entirely possible that some of your colleagues are better than you in sniffing out hidden flaws or weaknesses in people upon whom you all are going to depend if you are going to progress beyond the sandbox stage and really mother or father a company that is moving toward the big time. One reason Commandment One urged the formation of a *team* with consistent values was so that major decisions could be processed through various team members. Ask others to interview interesting candidates for key positions. Listen to your associates' opinions and reactions. Synthesize the evaluations. Every hiring decision entails some risk. The worst case is to get someone on board who is so-so. He or she is not good enough to promote and not bad enough to fire. By arranging multiple interviews and using your directors, advisors, other founders, and trusted confidants, you can minimize the risk in the always touchy art of evaluating people. Assessing a candidate's technical or functional capabilities is hard work. Once that work is done, the second side of the coin, the attitudinal or values side, comes up for thoughtful consideration.

There is an expanding body of literature on the phenomenon increasingly known as corporate or company culture. Any group of people who work together for awhile develop a culture. It typically includes certain accepted rules of behavior and a set of values. The explicit rules and values in a given company's culture may run the gamut from how to dress to how to deal with customer problems and subordinates. The *implicit* rules and values in an organization pick up where the explicit ones leave off. Over time, the combination of stated and unstated rules of behavior and values permeate a work force, for better or worse. They influence behavior. Behavior breeds more of the same, so norms develop. Newcomers violate such norms at their peril! Once again, every established company has a culture. Not every management team in the galaxy of established companies, however, has the corporate culture it wants.

Experience indicates that it is quite difficult to greatly change a culture once it has a firm foothold. Logic suggests that the ideal approach for an alert, progressive growth-company management team is to consciously define a desired culture early in the life of the organization. From that point on, it is a matter of cultivating the targeted culture via the managers, supervisors, activities, and reward systems of the enterprise...and the type of people employed.

There is a growing list of major companies who are adopting a rather general policy of only hiring people at the entry-job level and only promoting from within. "We grow our own," is the underlying thesis. And it is clear that by growing your own, it is simpler to generate a defined, consistent culture across the enterprise. Take a look at the Disney Company sometime. Check out what new employees experience when they become a part of the team at Disneyland, for example. But a new venture can hardly invest time and money to develop its key people from scratch. It needs experienced help to execute the dictates of the business plan. So what's to be done?

The conflict between growing your own people and culture and needing people "now" who can perform expertly in a technical or functional sense their first day on the job is best resolved in two ways. First, the criteria for hiring must be broadened beyond the usual technical considerations. People with specific *values* must be sought at the same time as you are looking for a salesperson or an accounting supervisor with four years experience. Second, each new employee needs a minimum of eight hours of orientation during his or her first three months with the company. That's how the inherent conflict can be at least partially resolved. This combination approach takes time up front during which the entrepreneurs think through what they themselves are about. This approach takes time in the field to ferret out qualified people. This approach takes executive time month after month because only the top people in a rapidly growing company can do orientations and communciate rules and values so that they stick to the ribs.

CASE O. Three middle-aged men formed a company dedicated to the thesis that with an average product for a very narrow but sizeable market segment, noticeably superior customer service, and a forty-hour week for each of them, they could make a lot of money. Within four years their thesis had become reality. In that time they built a company with over a thousand employees. In addition, they had executed a public offering of stock at a very attractive price, and the stock price held up very well. Over half of the employees were involved with customer service in one way or another. Early on the three partners formulated their philosophy. Each and every new employee from about number 25 on was (and is) fed the company philosophy almost incessantly. The key elements in the founders' own words are as follows: *(case continued on next page)*

- Any and every company problem is your problem. Therefore, don't pass the buck or point a finger at someone else.
- Glitter on your own time. That is, don't worry about status symbols and showing off on the job.
- We price and sell service; our technology or products are merely buckets to carry it in.
- Let our customers take advantage of us.
- Finish and put your name on every task you start.
- Bake your pride into what you do.
- We will pace company growth to personal growth.
- Simplicity rules here.
- Know what size shoes your customers wear.

A year ago two of the three founders retired for positive reasons to pursue other interests. People were promoted from within to replace those who had left. The company is continuing its dramatic, almost textbook growth. Unplanned turnover in the company is virtually zero.

CASE P. The management team of a successful, midwestern company has organized itself so that one of the four top officers is available for three hours each Monday morning to sit and talk with any employees hired during the past week. The meeting is loosely structured. The officers use some slides and flip chart pages, but mostly the officer puts herself or himself into the delivery, the orientation of the new people. The officers are currently considering expanding the effort so that all the company's employees have lunch with an officer at least once per year in small groups of six to ten people.

CASE Q. A two-year-old company in Southern California will only hire salespeople who have recently completed their college degrees at night or in a co-op, work-study program. According to the president: "We find that people with such backgrounds are twice as tenacious and productive as other

(case continued on next page)

sorts of people we have tried. They seem to fit into our particular culture and the way we operate here." She went on: "We believe in twelve-hour days with a long vacation once a year to recharge our batteries. We want salespeople who are comfortable with this pace."

In summary, technical and functional skills are only part of what it takes to build a large company from scratch. A new enterprise must have people with needed skills in its early days. An enterpreneur misses an important opportunity, however, if he or she doesn't also look for properly skilled people who want more than a job. The best way to judge what a person can do and wants is to assess their actions in the recent past. Once a new person is onboard, he or she influences—and is influenced by—the unfolding culture. It takes a conscious effort on the part of an entrepreneur to define, cultivate and maintain a discrete culture as new members join the company. It takes an investment of time and energy. Without such an investment, a culture will still develop. But it may serve as an anchor rather than a sail for the enterprise.

Setting Standards; Rewarding Performance

▼

THE SIXTH COMMANDMENT

REWARD INDIVIDUAL PERFOR-
MANCE THAT EXCEEDS AGREED
UPON STANDARDS.

Performance above the perfunctory level is a discretionary matter for each employee. Most people have alternative, off-the-job ways of utilizing excess energy or talent. Channeling such excess into activity beneficial to the business requires a tailored approach to each individual. A manager must first ensure that there is an understanding of the minimum results to be achieved. Then, for performance above the minimums, forms of compensation important to the performer–or in some cases, teams of performers–must be used.

Commandment One spoke to the importance of consistency among the primary participants in a new enterprise. Commandment Five suggested action to promulgate a conscious value orientation throughout an organization as it expands, recognizing full well that diversity will increase with success and size. Commandment Six calls for a sharp break with the past in that it admonishes the builders of new companies to do away with general, all-purpose reward systems.

People work for many reasons. This has always been the case. But winning bread is not the common denominator it once was. Today's work force is constructed of an incredible collection of individuals from all walks of life, each more liberated in one way or another than he or she would have been even ten years ago. Management people must seek to align the efforts of individuals with the vision, mission, and objectives of the organization as a whole. It is folly to think that general profit sharing plans or benefits packages or promotion criteria or a quarterly beer blast or arty pictures in the lobby or Friday-after-work schmoozing are going to stimulate or reinforce desired behavior right across the population of the enterprise. Once again...*forms of compensation important to the performer–or in some cases, teams of performers–must be used.*

Conventional wisdom suggests that every employee wants to get rich, be promoted into positions of larger responsibility, have his or her medical expenses paid, work in pleasant surroundings, have a nice boss, be fulfilled, and retire with a substantial nest egg. Much of this thinking by corporate pacesetters is unconsiously based on Abraham Maslow's famous 1940s hierarchy-of-needs paradigm.

Maslow postulated that people have a progression, a hierarchy, of needs, starting at the bottom with physiological needs and moving upwards. As a given need level becomes satisfied, a new need emerges that drives or motivates the individual until that need is reasonably filled. This process goes onward and upward—a continuing sequence all the way to the open-ended top level, the need for self-actualization. Maslow's hierarchy has provided the theoretical underpinnings for a great deal of what has gone on under the heading of motivation and personnel work over the past fifty years. It replaced piece-

Maslow's Hierarchy of Needs

Self-actualization—personal fulfillment

Recognition as an individual

Status needs—identity with a group

Safety needs—security, health

Physiological needs—food, shelter, warmth

work as the secret to what makes employees tick. The question for entrepreneurs is, does it fit the realities of the 1990s and beyond? At least one modern researcher, Daniel Yankelovich, thinks not.

Maslowism: The Biggest Trap of All*

The quest for self-fulfillment borrows its forms of expression from whatever sources are most convenient. Unfortunately, the materials closest to hand have been an odd combination of the psychology of affluence, reinforced by an outlook whose interwoven tenets proclaim: live for

*From New Rules-Searching for Self-fulfillment in a World Turned Upside Down by Daniel Yankelovich. Copyright © 1981 by Daniel Yankelovich. Reprinted by permission of Random House, Inc.

the moment, regard the self as a sacred object, be more self-assertive, hold nothing back. Where did those assumptions come from?

Early in the postwar quarter-century, the ideas of "more of everything" and the "primacy of self" merged in a school of thought that may be called "self" psychology. Self psychology received its most influential expression in the work of the psychologists Abraham H. Maslow, Carl Rogers, and Erich Fromm. Their thinking spread throughout the culture, with the help of self-help movements such as est and books with titles such as Looking Out for No. 1, How to Be Your Own Best Friend, *and* Pulling Your Own Strings.

In particular, the theories of Maslow ingeniously combine a psychology of affluence with a vision of inner development. In the 1950s, Maslow posited a hierarchy of human needs that has become part of the conventional wisdom of our time. According to the hierarchy, people who are preoccupied with meeting "lower-order needs" for food, shelter, and economic security have little energy left for pursuing the "higher-order needs" of the spirit. Vital energies are released to the search for "self-actualization" only when the lower-order needs have been met. We move up the hierarchy of needs in an orderly fashion, on an escalator of increasing affluence.

There is obviously some sense in which human priorities do function according to a hierarchy. When we are sick, all that counts is getting well. When our survival, physical or economic, is threatened, it powerfully concentrates the mind (as Samuel Johnson observed about the prospect of being hanged). But the idea of self-actualization–the highest achievement of which human beings are capable, according to Maslow–presupposes our ascension through various stages of economic well-being and is a peculiarly self-congratulatory philosophy for a materialistic age.

In Maslowism, the self-actualized person who steps off at the top of the escalator is a particular personality type. He or she is assumed to be a creative, autonomous self, virtually independent of culture. The theme of the creative individual, independent of culture, is to be repeated over and over again in the literature of self psychology and its pop-psychology progeny. One of Wayne Dyer's books speaks glowingly of the theory that "you are the sum total of your choices."

By now, millions of Americans have garnered extensive—and painful—experience in personal struggles with the new, Maslow-inspired duty-to-self ethic. It has, to be sure, some benefits to offer the individual, but the core idea is a moral and social absurdity. It gives moral sanction to desires that do not contribute to society's well-being. It contains no principle for synchronizing the requirements of the society with the goals of the individual. It fails to discriminate between socially valuable desires and socially destructive ones, and often works perversely against the real goals of both individuals and society. It provides no principle other than hedonism for interpreting the meaning of the changes and sacrifices we must make to adapt to new economic-political conditions.

Where does this leave the entrepreneur? Conventional wisdom says everyone wants to strive upwards; the economic and social reality of these, our times, suggests that such wisdom is fast becoming obsolete. As an alternative, here is a sequence of thinking that experience indicates will work as the year 2000 approaches. First, an entrepreneur needs to consciously recognize that an important part of his or her work as a founder/manager is to help other people succeed in the organization. The aspiring entrepreneur has to appreciate that a significant portion of time must be devoted to being a coach rather than being a player. And as the enterprise grows, the percentage of time devoted to coaching will probably gradually increase for most members of the management team. Graphically, the progression looks like this:

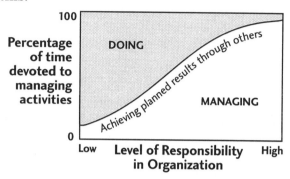

The inability of entrepreneurs to reallocate their time and energy, to manage more and "do" less, is one of the most common reasons why many young enterprises stall just as they start to succeed. More on this in Commandment Ten. A second step in the sequence of thinking is to establish agreed upon standards of performance with those directly involved. The overwhelming evidence turned up by both academics and practitioners over the years is that people tend to respond to structured expectations. They need to know—want to know—where is the goal line or fence? What is the name of the game or the shape of the target? How high is up? What are the acceptable minimum results? What do you expect of me? Lest you think these phrases are merely cliches, spend some time chatting with a cross section of employees in a lunchroom or two. Ask about their everyday concerns; listen carefully to their vocabulary. People on the job want to know what is expected of them. As one engineer put it, "I can't operate in the dark."

The point is that the practice of managing with objectives covered in Commandment Three has to be percolated down through an organization to the individual employee level. Corporate objectives become meaningful when they are translated into what it is that a given man or woman is to achieve in, say, the next thirty, sixty, or ninety days.

The third step in the sequence of working with employees is to insure that the reward systems and practices of the enterprise support and reinforce the desired behavior of the individual(s) involved.

CASE R. The management team of a young specialty chemicals company with operations in six locations across the United States was interested in steadily increasing the company's sales volume and, at the same time, decreasing the salesforce expenses—absolutely and as a percentage of sales. The management team also espoused decentralized decision making. The president finally settled on a system that a) effectively raised the salespeople's commission on orders obtained and shipped in their well-defined territories, and b) gave each salesperson precisely $500 a month for expenses, no more and no less. This shifted operating decisions about travel, entertainment, how to spend time, and whether to stay overnight at a Hilton and eat a steak dinner to the individual in the field. If a salesperson spent less than the $500 for expenses in a given month, he or she pocketed the difference as income. And it was he or she who had to weigh the cost of any sales and sales commissions lost by *under*spending on travel and entertainment. If a salesperson wanted to spend more than $500 a month, he or she could spend it—out of his or her own pocket.

The company is continuing to grow at a five-year compound rate of over 60 percent. Salesforce turnover has been very low. Salesforce expenses are down, absolutely and as a percentage of sales.

Not everybody is driven by money. Dual promotion ladders whereby individuals can advance in status, responsibility and income without moving into managing jobs are becoming more common, especially in higher technology companies. In many phases of science and engineering it's almost a full-time job today just to keep current. To compound that burden with the additional tasks of getting results through others invites both frustration and, perhaps, failure. Entrepreneurial innovations in organizational design and organizational processes can be as important as technical breakthroughs.

CASE S. The founder/managers of an exciting new entry in the business-machine field decreed early on that the company would have no dead-end jobs. Today the company has sales exceeding $100 million. It has no private secretaries, but it does have a very state-of-the-art, multipurpose, internal communications system. The company has no janitors or guards; it does have subcontractors who provide these services. Each new employee is guaranteed a job change opportunity within two years of his or her starting date as well as three performance appraisals during the interim. No profit center (operating business unit) can exceed 500-700 employees without becoming a candidate for division into two or more profit centers. The company farms out all manufacturing and subassembly work that is expected to become standardized and routine.

Can the management of Case S hold to its no dead-end jobs principle when the company has 5,000 and then 10,000 employees? Time will tell, but management attention *will* be required.

For many reasons, working people increasingly look to their employers to respond to a broader range of human needs than in the past. This phenomenon presents entrepreneurial managers and executives with one of their greatest opportunities. It may also present them with a duty, but for certain there is an opportunity.

The opportunity is to make the modern corporation an integral and imaginative part of the evolving social fabric of the times. Most of the larger, established companies of today were formed and shaped before the 1960s. The burst of entrepreneurial activity in the late 1960s was largely technologically based. The renaissance of entrepreneuring in the 1980s and 1990s has a much broader foundation, one that reflects the passing of the traditional industrialism with its steel mills, assembly lines, and relatively small percentage of college-educated adults in the work force.

The new entrepreneurialism is based on a pluralistic, global society with many discrete, unique markets. It is based on a population of knowledge workers who are wired together in an infinite variety of ways. And it is based on the enduring need for human contact and relationships, not in spite of the march toward individual recognition, but in addition to it.

Now all the evidence of psychiatry . . . shows that membership in a group sustains a man, enables him to maintain his equilibrium under the ordinary shocks of life, and helps him to bring up children who will in turn be happy and resilient. If his group is shattered around him, if he leaves a group in which he was a valued member, and if, above all, he finds no new group to which he can relate himself, he will under stress, develop disorders of thought, feeling, and behavior . . . The cycle is vicious; loss of group membership in one generation may make men less capable of group membership in the next. The civilization that, by its very process of growth, shatters small group life will leave men and women lonely and unhappy.

George C. Homans, The Human Group*

Entrepreneuring is more than capitalizing on an opportunity spawned by knowledge and the times. It is a force for change and human development that transcends any particular product, service, or market opening at a point in history.

*William G. Ouchi and Alfred M. Jaeger, "Type Z Organization: A Corporate Alternative to Village Life." *Stanford Business School Alumni Bulletin,* Fall 1977-1978, p. 13.

Walk Before You Run

THE SEVENTH COMMANDMENT

> EXPAND METHODICALLY FROM
> A PROFITABLE BASE TOWARD A
> BALANCED BUSINESS.

Optimism is both the poison and the antidote of the growth company manager. It may be possible to accomplish all things, but not simultaneously. With limited resources, incremental growth over time is the judicious prescription for prosperity. Seek logical, extensions of existing activities, but avoid a growth-for-growth's-sake psychology. Bigger is not automatically better; more is not necessarily merrier. Make managing a competitive advantage. Increase customer dependency on the enterprise. Economic success can breed more of the same as well as other returns for the primary participants. Money is the traditional reward; life-style considerations are becoming more widely valued.

Walk before you run. Don't build your skyscraper on sand. Sometimes you have to bunt to get on first base. Avoid growing into trouble. Measure twice, cut once. All of these aphorisms tend to ring true in the cold light of day. But historically, expanding methodically has proven to be something of an unnatural act for those who grow new companies . . . and even sometimes for experienced entrepreneurs who try to turn around old ones. A few years back, Roy Ash, cofounder of Litton Industries and later director of the Office of Management and Budget in Washington, D.C., was fired as the chairman and chief executive officer of the money-losing AM International (formerly called Addressograph-Multigraph). As reported in *Fortune:*

". . . Ash's big blunder was his failure to build a solid foundation of profits before making acquisitions."

How does an entrepreneur protect himself or herself from the harmful side effects of optimism, the tendency to see an opportunity under every rock? First and foremost, he or she must have a deep sensitivity to the mechanics of profitability–to basic profit math.

"We expect to make 20 percent on sales." "Our new program is going to give us 30 percent before taxes." "Product A will make money every day of the year." These kinds of common statements reflect an important and widespread misconception that goes like this: Every dollar of sales has a portion of profit in it. Here's the picture:

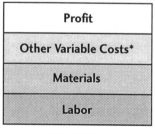

$1 of Sales

* Note: Variable costs are those costs that vary with volume, e.g., some labor, raw materials, freight, sales commissions, packaging, etc.

Look familiar? The problem is, of course, that it is wrong. There are no pennies of profit in any $1 of Sales until *all* the fixed costs of the enterprise are covered. A much more useful way to illustrate the situation is this:

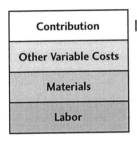

Contribution to:
1) fixed costs, and then
2) profit requirements

For example, if the fixed costs like many salaries, rent, insurance, etc. of a venture are projected to be $100,000 for the first year in business, no profit will be made until the $100,000 is covered.

The mechanics of profitability can handily be summed up and illustrated by the following graph, a graph that at various times goes under the name of break-even chart and profit-volume chart.

The vertical axis is profit; the horizontal axis is sales volume. At zero sales, the amount of profit is a negative number, a loss! The loss is equal to the fixed cost of the time period under study.

If each unit sold and sales dollar received does indeed have a contribution (defined in more detail below), then the fixed cost is gradually whittled away until the enterprise "breaks even." After that point, the contribution from each unit sold and sales dollar received goes totally to profit.

Here is the idea expressed in formulas:

Sales Price - Variable Costs = Contribution per sales $ or unit of sales

Fixed Costs ÷ Contribution = Break-even Point in terms of sales $ or units

Total Sales Income - (Total Variable Costs + Fixed Costs) = Profit

Now, for the purposes of Commandment Seven, the important issue to recognize is that there are three fundamental elements in the profitability of a company:

Sales Volume...in units or dollars

Fixed Costs...for the time period

Contribution...per unit of sale or sales dollar

For example, suppose you are working on a new venture with these essential facts:

First year's fixed costs are projected to be $550,000
Sales price of your product is projected to be $100 per unit
Variable cost of product is projected to be $45 per unit

Try graphing the above information in an effort to answer these questions:

How many units will have to be sold to break even?
What will be the sales volume in dollars at the break-even point?
How much profit will the company make if it sells 25,000 units during the first year?

Do your work on the graph on the following page.

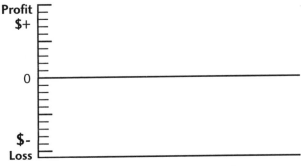

The math works out as follows:

Sales Price $100
Variable Costs ..... -45
Contribution .... $55 per unit.

$$\frac{\text{Fixed Cost}}{\text{Contribution}} = \frac{\$550,000}{\$55 / \text{Unit}} = 10,000 \text{ units} \atop \text{to break even.}$$

Graphically the above information can be presented like this:

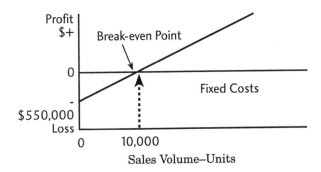

The sales volume at 10,000 units is 10,000 x $100 sales price per unit or $1 million. The new venture will have to reach $1 million in sales volume before it starts making a profit.

If the entrepreneurs can sell 25,000 units, an amount well above the break-even point, the profit will be as follows:

$2,500,000 Sales Income - ($1,125,000 Variable Costs + $550,000 Fixed Cost) = $825,000.

At a sales volume of 25,000 units, the profit picture looks like this:

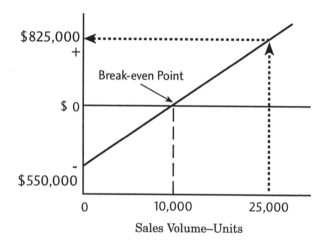

Not bad! Now here is one important refinement to understanding these basics. In actual practice, the contribution is usually converted to a percentage, a contribution *rate*.

$$\frac{\text{Contribution per unit}}{\text{Sales Price per unit}} = \text{Contribution Rate}$$

In this example, the contribution rate was:

$$\frac{\$55}{\$100} = 55\%$$

Graphically the contribution percentage looks like this:

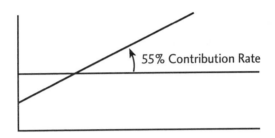

In effect what this picture says is that 55 percent out of every sales dollar is available to pay first, for the fixed costs and second, for the profit *requirements* of the enterprise. In a growth company, profit is indeed a requirement, not a luxury.

Think back over the ground that has been covered here in Commandment Seven. The crux of the matter of profitability fundamentals is simply this: An entrepreneurial team can harm—or kill—profitability by trying to do too much, too soon. For what often happens when opportunity chasing overrules methodical growth is that overhead (fixed costs) goes up and the contribution rate comes down. This is a dangerous turn of events. The end result may well be greater sales volume for the enterprise, but it is paid for with eroding profitability. The combination of higher fixed costs and dropping contribution margin is typically not a formula for long-term happiness!

Consider the following example of sales and profits for the Widgetronics Company, Inc.

	1990	1991	1992
Sales	$1,000,000	$3,000,000	$10,000,000
Profits	$100,000	$200,000	0

Upon analysis, the deterioration of Widgetronic's profitability can be illustrated. (You don't have the figures to do the analysis, but please note the factors driving profitability down.)

In table form, the analysis looked like this:

	1990	1991	1992
Sales	$1,000,000	$3,000,000	$10,000,000
Profits	$100,000	$200,000	0
Fixed Costs	$300,000	$550,000	$1,000,000
Variable Costs	$600,000	$2,250,000	$9,000,000
Contribution Rate	40%	25%	10%
Break-even Point	$750,000	$2,200,000	$10,000,000

The company is going downhill quite dramatically.

What did Widgetronics' management do between 1990 and 1992? Certainly the team increased sales.

"Look at our 300 percent growth over last year!" But in the process, the fixed costs tripled, and perhaps more importantly, the contribution rate was allowed to drop precipitously from forty cents per sales dollar to ten cents. By 1992, Widgetronics had to sell $10 million of business just to *break even* at year end. Unless there are compelling strategic reasons to do so and plenty of money to play with, such performance is unacceptable in the turbulent nineties.

An even more detailed analysis of how Widgetronics grew itself into trouble indicates that between 1990 and 1992 the management added two major new product lines, one closely related to the main business and one not. Here are the highlights of the impact the additions had on the contribution rate and the fixed costs. Note carefully what the new, unrelated product line brought to Widgetronics.

Original Product Line	1990	1991	1992
Sales	$1,000,000	$2,000,000	$ 4,000,000
Contribution Rate	40%	30%	40%
Associated Fixed Costs	$ 300,000	$ 300,000	$ 400,000
New Product Line (Related)			
Sales	0	$ 500,000	$ 2,000,000
Contribution Rate		20%	10%
Associated Fixed Costs		$ 100,000	$ 200,000
New Product Line (Unrelated)			
Sales	0	$ 500,000	$ 4,000,000
Contribution Rate		10%	−20%*
Associated Fixed Costs		$ 150,000	$ 400,000

*Variable costs exceeded selling price

Totals for Widgetronics			
Sales	$1,000,000	$3,000,000	$10,000,000
Contribution Rate	40%	25%	10%
Fixed Costs	$ 300,000	$ 550,000	$ 1,000,000
Break-even Point	$ 750,000	$2,200,000	$10,000,000
Profits	$ 100,000	$ 200,000	0

In this hypothetical example, a combination of factors hurt the profitability of the company in 1992. New, unrelated product lines are not categorically troublemakers. But they should be approached with caution and detailed planning.

If you personally are not comfortable working with and manipulating numbers in the way illustrated above, make sure at least one of the primary participants on your entrepreneurial team is!

As in any business, Widgetronics management has but three basic ways to increase the profitability of the enterprise. They can seek to increase sales volume (of products with positive contribution rates), reduce fixed costs, or increase the contribution rate. And there are also three specific ways to increase the contribution rate:

- Increase selling prices.
- Decrease variable costs.
- Change the product mix being sold so as to increase the net contribution rate for all products being sold.

Of course, in the Widgetronics example, as in real life, a combination of actions is probably required.

Profits don't just happen. Like sales, they typically have to be made to happen. Entrepreneurs must have a sensitivity to the dynamics involved. Profitability isn't a luxury; it is a necessity in a growth company. Without it there are no earnings to "retain." Without earnings on today's business it is usually difficult to attract either equity or debt capital to finance tomorrow's business. Profitability is the progenitor of cash, and when you are out of cash, you increasingly tend to be out for good in these undulating economic times.

Entrepreneurs are naturally disposed toward spotting opportunities in the form of new product possibilities, additional markets to pursue, processes to initiate, exciting shortcuts to take, etc. Entrepreneurs move society from the old to the new. But a fragile new enterprise will be lucky if the people there can do a single thing exceptionally well and consistently during the early years. It may be possible to accomplish all things, but not simultaneously. As one weary president put it, "We can do anything, but we can't do everything." With limited resources, incremental growth over time is the judicious prescription for prosperity.

Go With the (Cash) Flow

THE EIGHTH COMMANDMENT

> PROJECT, MONITOR, AND CONSERVE CASH AND CREDIT CAPABILITY.

Cash is the blood of a growth business. A company's ability to continue is determined daily by the contents of the checking account, not at year's end by the financial statement. Keeping money in hand or readily available for both planned and unplanned events is not only prudent but necessary in unsettled times. Cultivation of financial sources is an ongoing duty.

Probably no other commandment is violated more broadly and regularly than this one. Cash gets consumed in many ways, some of them quite unexpected. In recent years steady growth, roller-coaster interest rates, a fickle government in Washington, D.C., and spooky markets for new stock and debt offerings have driven even the largest corporations into wild new patterns of financing themselves. Many of the new patterns involve sophisticated financing schemes that only a chosen few can decipher. As chronicled in the *Wall Street Journal, Fortune, Forbes, Business Week,* and elsewhere, new instruments like derivatives have resulted in big bruises on organizations as diverse as Procter & Gamble and Orange County, California. At one point in the last decade, interest expense alone consumed nearly 45 percent of corporate net profit before taxes, up from only 14 percent in the 1960s, according to Henry Kaufman, the chief economist at Salomon Brothers. Kaufman has also written that, "Getting hooked on short-term debt has made U.S. corporations more vulnerable to recession than at any time since the 1930s."

The squeeze on cash for operations due to a jump in interest rates on borrowings is one example of how an unplanned event can cripple a company, regardless of size. A second cash sump that periodically catches high growth company managements napping is inventory. A few years back scores of semiconductor companies found themselves with months and months of product on hand and no customers. The cash accounts on their balance sheets dwindled; the inventory accounts ballooned. But you can't meet a payroll with inventory. More than one emerging company has found it necessary to let key people go, a high price to pay for failing to protect cash reserves as a market cools or the economy slows.

The third great cash consumer tends to be accounts receivable, the money your customers owe you. Without intending to do so, many entrepreneurs start out being a manufacturer or service-provider and end up being a bank (of sorts)!

CASE T. A young, well-degreed couple started a consulting business aimed at cashing in on the booming racquetball, squash, and indoor tennis market. They offered a full range of services based on their own backgrounds and athletic prowess. They could give a client a turn-key package, everything from court layout and building design to retail merchandise selection and club management procedures. The couple did very well during their first two years in business. They even expanded into wholesaling certain types of equipment–special shoes and racquets, clothing for left-handers, etc. In their third year they got their "big break"–a contract with a major land developer to do a chain of twelve racquet complexes in five southwestern cities. The contract required concentrated effort stretching over a fifteen-month period. The two consultants worked very hard and billed the developer for fees and expenses at the end of each month. When they had not received any payments after the third month, they expressed some concern to their client. He assured them the delay was strictly administrative and that a check was in the mail. A month later they received a check for the first month. But no more checks were forthcoming. By the end of the sixth month the couple had invoices outstanding of over $150,000, and they had incurred over $35,000 in out-of-pocket expenses for lodging, food, and continuous travel to the client's twelve sites. The client repeatedly assured them the delay was only temporary.

The couple engaged an attorney. She went after the developer. He fired the two consultants. They went to court. In the meantime, their successful, pre-big break consulting business was derailed due to lack of attention. To date, eighteen months later, they still haven't collected a portion of the money they claim they are due. But they still show it on their balance sheet in accounts receivable.

Is there a moral to the story? Yes. Watch out when you start extending credit. Don't become a finance company unintentionally.

Usually, the management of a new enterprise assumes that it must conform to the prevailing practices of the industry or industries in which it will operate. If the industry standard is to allow *net thirty days* on the payment of invoices, then the entrepreneurs allow net thirty days. Doing so is very understandable. But two questions should be asked. One, if the new company does indeed have a better mousetrap of some sort, does it need to meet the industry standard? Perhaps tighter terms can be sold. Two, what actions will be taken if whatever terms adopted are violated by customers—as in Case T above?

Many entrepreneurs shy away from these types of administrative issues. They are hardly the stuff dreams are made of, particularly in the early days of a new venture when everyone is aglow with visions of empires, self-fulfillment, service to society, capital gains, or all of the above. But, honored reader, you are admonished to recognize the cold fact that a business without cash is like a sailboat without wind. Depending upon who's aboard, sitting dead in the water, windless, may be interesting, even fun, for awhile. But at some point, survival becomes an issue. Projecting, monitoring, and conserving cash is not an optional feature of entrepreneuring. It is the major part of a high-level, heavyweight task for one of the primary participants. Another part of that task is the continuing cultivation of financial sources.

The thrust of this book has been toward building growth companies. Almost by definition, growth companies usually need more money than they can generate internally. That incremental money has to come from outside. The range of normal outside sources is pretty well known:

Individual investors (the public)
Private investors (wealthy individuals)
Professional investment funds (venture capitalists)
Foundations (money for special causes)
Corporations (joint ventures and equity investments)
Creditors (banks, SBA, individuals)
Credit companies (accounts receivable financing)
Suppliers (extended payment terms)
Customers (payments in advance)
Employees (stock purchases, wage/salary concessions)

Chances are that sooner or later you will have to rely on one or more of these ten sources to supply some additional wind for your sails. The time to go after money is before you need it!

It is a well-known phenomenon that it's relatively easy to get a loan, for example, when you've already got plenty of cash on hand. In such circumstances your credit is five-star (or AAA) and any creditor has little worry about getting repaid. It follows that the time to cultivate relations with potential future sources of capital is when you are doing well, meeting your plan, and running smoothly. Essentially what the entrepreneur must do is build confidence on the part of others—confidence in his or her management team, the business concept, and the future of the combination. How is this efficiently done? Pick one or two target sources from the list of ten and court them from day one.

One of the key products of your business plan, your blueprint, is a thoughtful indication of how much money is required at various points along the way in the early years of the business. The business plan, or more likely, updated versions of it, can be your basic tool in courting potential sources of initial as well as later rounds of financing. Let your targeted individuals read the plan. Ask for comments. Then keep the intended investors and creditors informed of your progress.

In addition, include your targeted sources in periodic mailings. Visit them. Draw them into the life of the company in ways convenient to you. Should you let your potential sources of future debt or equity know why you are cultivating them? Of course! You're not playing a game with your business. You are going after needed funding in the same way you would go after needed raw materials or vital parts or a person you would like very much to hire. There's nothing sacred about money. It just happens to have more mystique than other business ingredients. Go after it. There's generally more money around than there are good, thought-out business ideas and plans. Once you've done your homework, figure "they" need you more than you need them. This is not to suggest arrogance on your part, merely conviction.

There is evidence of the dawn of a new day for progressive business management. The old day featured a rapidly growing population, apparently unlimited natural resources, cheap energy, a stable currency, low interest rates and low inflation, relative isolation from overseas competition, and a compliant work force that understood hard times. The new day features just the opposite. And the hard times of the transition to the new day are especially aggravating to the most recent generation of employees who had come to take good times, economically speaking, for granted. As the dawn gives way to the new day, managers in general and entrepreneurs in particular have to deal skillfully with the fundamentals of business.

Customer service is already a battle cry across the nation. The effective linking and full use of talent at all organizational levels is becoming fashionable, but it will receive increasing attention as the year 2000 approaches and passes. Marketing will be tightened up in many ways. For example, the proliferation of me-too products will fade as the buying public increasingly seeks real value, rather than the cosmetic appearance of value. Production processes are already undergoing a revolution. Purchasing has increased markedly in stature as a vital business function. Finance now is a global activity that never sees a sunset. The Internet and the information highway, or "farmer's market" as it is called by Microsoft's Bill Gates, are opening whole new vistas of opportunity for those around the world who have their antennas raised. In this time of seemingly unlimited opportunity, cash will continue to be the life blood of a growth business. Entrepreneurs by nature tend to favor hard cash over paper assets anyway. The new day, the new century, is made for them.

Health is Wealth

THE NINTH COMMANDMENT

MAINTAIN A DETACHED POINT OF VIEW.

Managing a growing business requires unyielding dedication that can consume the body, impair the senses, and warp the mind. Such effects are harmful to the individual and the enterprise. Clinical objectivity is the only preventive. Growth implies and entails risk. Risk begets failure as well as successes. Wide perspective gained through nonbusiness experience or study helps one endure the pressures and accept with equanimity the results, good and bad, of business decisions.

Few new ventures get very far without a lot of what is termed "sweat equity," the investment of many, many long days of toil by the key people. Just why this investment seems to be mandatory is unclear. It may be a law of the universe. It may have something to do with giving birth to a new entity. The explanation may reside with the fact that entrepreneurs typically have sizeable egos, so they try to do everything themselves. Whatever the cause, when there is an *excessive* amount of sweat equity invested over time by one or more individuals, the size, success, and overall health of the total enterprise is going to be at risk.

CASE U. Sam J., aged thirty-six, was hired away from a large electronics firm to be the general manager of a startup company. The company was founded and financed by two older, private investors and a venture capital fund. The company did well and within a year Sam was made president. During that year fourteen-hour days were the norm for Sam as he hired, fired, sold, billed, designed, cajoled, figured, and, on occasion, worked on the production line. Sam was the hub of the wheel, and as the company grew, he took great pride in being on a first-name basis with every employee and issue. The company prospered, but by the third year Sam was clearly stretched too thin. His board prevailed on him to add three vice-presidents. He did, but for the most part they were not strong people. Probably subconsciously, Sam tended to hire dependent subordinates so that his position as the hub remained undisturbed.

The flourishing company sold stock to the public and moved into its own new factory during its fourth year. That same year Sam and his wife built a new home high on a hill near the factory. The axis of the new home was aligned with the factory, and the living room bay window looked directly down on it. Sam often invited groups of employees other than his officers to dinner. He invited the officers, too, on occasion. The dinners were one of the many ways Sam was

(case continued on next page)

able to keep his finger on the pulse of the operation and perpetuate his network of information sources within the company. Sam continued his twelve-to-fourteen-hour days. Everyone felt he set an excellent example.

The growth of the company slowed in its fifth year. Sam took it quite personally and chided his vice-presidents to work harder. The problems which seemed to be overtaking the company included a lack of new products, a rather primitive accounting and control system, aging production processes, and weak marketing. Sam attacked all of the problems. A downturn in the economy aggravated the situation. At that point Sam became desperate. During one week he fired two vice-presidents, signed a $200,000 contract with a consulting firm to diagnose the company's situation, and triggered a violent oral exchange with the two founders regarding the source of the company's fall from grace in terms of performance.

Within four months the founders had sold their sizeable block of the company to an acquisition-minded conglomerate. The conglomerate picked up the rest of the stock of the company at a bargain price six months later.

Was Sam a hero or a villain? A very thin line separates the two in the world of entrepreneuring. He gave the enterprise what it needed in the early days. He gave it all he had. In the process, his personality became inseparable from the business itself, and the vital element of objectivity was lost. People didn't work for the company; they worked for Sam. Sam wasn't the president of a growth venture, the captain of the company's management team. He was a self-appointed king of the realm. The company didn't fail; it outgrew its leadership and then collapsed when the single hub could no longer support the weight of the enlarged wheel.

Sam's inability to step back and put some distance between himself and the enterprise is a common problem. It is particularly visible at the entrepreneurial end of the sequence of stages through which most successful companies pass. In recent years, scholars have analyzed a cross-section of companies in an effort to discover any distinct and recurring growth patterns. Most notable among the efforts was a comprehensive study done by Professor Larry E. Greiner at the University of Southern California. It supported the conclusion that, indeed, many companies pass through some common stages and crisis points. An appreciation for the stages and crises can assist top managers in piloting their enterprises over time. The highlights in the corporate metamorphosis are illustrated in the diagram below.*

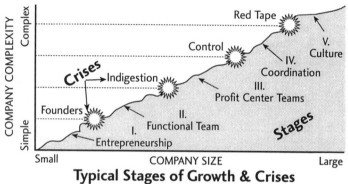

Typical Stages of Growth & Crises

As companies become older and larger (x-axis), they usually also become more complex (y-axis) because of either product line or market expansion, or both. As a given company becomes more complex, the managing practices used by the key people need to change; often the structure of the company has to change as well. Stage one in the diagram, growth through **Entrepreneurship**, is the subject of this book. Here, one person or a small group works long, hard, informally, and quickly to launch a new enterprise. A certain percentage of startups succeed *because* of the energy applied. But the single-minded dedication of the early executives often also contains the

---

* Adapted from article by Larry E. Greiner, "Evolution and Revolution as Organizations Grow," *Harvard Business Review,* July-August 1972, p. 41.

seeds for the first crisis: the **Founders** crisis. The entrepreneur tries to do everything himself or herself; he or she won't let go of some of the reins; the company's needs exceed the grasp of the one or two individuals in the driver's seat; the enterprise bumps off the road to success.

What does it take to stay on the upward growth curve, to continue succeeding beyond what is typically the first crisis point? Usually it takes a broadening of the management talent base, some effective staffing that adds up to the well-rounded **Functional Team** needed for stage two growth. Such a team might include accounting or manufacturing or marketing experts depending on the needs of the business and the voids in the entrepreneur's expertise. In this second stage the entrepreneur, if he or she is to make the transition personally, must begin getting results through others as opposed to through his or her own individual efforts. Many entrepreneurs find this a tough transition to make, and many don't make it. Sam in Case U above illustrates this point.

In companies where this leadership hurdle is cleared, progress up the growth curve often continues. Products and markets are typically added; the business prospers and also becomes rapidly more complex. The stage is set for the second major crisis, **Centralization**. The single level of general management normally found in a functional organization gets to the point where it simply can no longer efficiently handle the increasingly diverse issues, problems, and questions flooding in from the various functional vice-presidents. (Refer to section 6.0 in the material on Preparing a Business Plan, Commandment Four.) General management suffers an overload. People miss schedules and overrun budgets. Communications bog down. Silly mistakes are made. And the quality of decisions at the top declines because the distance between the general management and the realities at the customer interface has become too great. The enterprise is suffering from success. Usually the best medicine is to break the company into smaller, more manageable pieces–to decentralize into **Profit Center Teams.**

Stage three growth, with its multiple profit centers, means that at least one additional layer of general management is added to the organization. This puts key decisions closer to the customer interface. It is often also true that now there will be a more homogeneous character to the range of issues with which each profit center team must deal, since profit centers are typically formed around a single product line, geographical area, or type of customer. Stage three growth, however, like the other stages, carries with it the seeds of the next crisis. The varied actions of independent profit centers breed the crisis of **Control**.

Profit center teams have a tendency to go off in their own directions. When this happens, the total enterprise becomes merely the sum of the parts instead of more than the sum. Corporate management gets increasingly uneasy as it senses that it's losing touch with what is going on. The objectives of the enterprise become fuzzy as it is stretched in several directions. Overall, things get out of control. The people at the center of the complexity can't spell out for sure what business they are in. **Coordination** is needed in order to exploit competitive advantages systematically on a company-wide basis. Such coordination, stage four of growth, usually takes the form of added management information systems and progress reporting mechanisms, and a more rigorous planning schedule throughout the year. In short, more meetings, manuals, and memos–the bane of the traditional entrepreneur!

These adjustments, in time, do bring about a higher

degree of coordination. Experience indicates that they also can usher in the next crisis, **Red Tape**. The busy business builders in the emerging profit centers find they are spending two-thirds of their time justifying what they do during the remaining third. The control systems developed for the decentralized company become anchors instead of sails. How is the red tape cut, or thinned, without letting the pieces of the enterprise fly apart again? A variety of human overrides to control systems have been tried. Examples include task forces, matrix structures, and administrative maneuvers to promote the productive interaction of seasoned people for the good of the whole organization. These overrides are sometimes successful, but as a rule they are not particularly enduring. For example, how long can a task force prevail on a subject? A fresh slant on how to accomplish optimal coordination in companies with increasingly diverse activities (products/services/markets/technologies) is to try to *internalize* the values, checks, and balances in at least the key players. Such internalization suggests the development of a corporate **Culture**, a term introduced in Commandment Five. The existence of a culture implies that a group of people share a point of view about matters important to a larger enterprise of which they are a part. For more on how to accomplish this, see *The Art of Japanese Management,* referenced earlier in Commandment Four. You may also want to see *Theory Z* by William Ouchi.*

A key point to remember is that the management practices that breed success at one stage (like the investment of sweat equity during the Entrepreneurship stage) carry with them the seeds for a crisis. *It is necessary for an entrepreneur to change his or her managing style as his or her company prospers.* What worked yesterday or today is not the formula for tomorrow. A sensitivity to this issue of managing style is essential if a

---

* William Ouchi *Theory Z–How American Business Can meet the Japanese Challenge* (Reading, Mass: Addison-Wesley, 1981)

person is to achieve the degree of clinical objectivity called for here in Commandment Nine.

What else is required? Good health, including adequate rest, and some semblance of a balance between vocational and avocational interests. Few people appreciate the physical wear and tear required to found and run a dynamic enterprise. Any busy manager or executive in any business can tally the litany of meetings, phone calls, airports, rent-a-cars, airplanes, hotel rooms, deadlines, and so forth that he or she endures. Now add to this litany the incremental burdens on entrepreneurs who have to initiate everything, work without staff support, and shoulder the stress of possibly being wrong or ineffective on a critical item at any given point in the day. The load on the individual, the entrepreneur, the person who is his or her own boss, is often essentially doubled.

The only antidote is physical and mental fitness equal to the load. Self-help books by the hundreds prescribe appropriate routines for getting and/or staying in shape. And any competent M.D., especially one associated with preventive medicine, the entrepreneurial end of medicine, can help you tailor-make a program compatible, within reason, with your own lifestyle. Likewise, regarding mental health, particularly stress, there is a growing body of knowledge about what causes stress and how to deal with it. A foremost authority in the matter is Dr. Hans Selye, M.D., professor emeritus at the University of Montreal and president of the International Institute of Stress.

Dr. Selye, among others, has pointed out that at its roots, stress results from the body trying to readjust or adapt itself to a new situation. The situation can be good or bad, real or imagined. This is a very important point to appreciate. Your body reacts measurably to each of the following kinds of events:

A threat by a mugger on a city street.
Receipt of a huge order for your company.
A death in the family.
Leaving on a vacation trip to Europe.
A sudden shortage of cash to pay bills.
The apparent failure of a key subordinate to
     meet expectations.
The loss of a major client.
Extensive, unexpected bad weather.

Each good, bad, real, or imagined event (the mugger may just be a shadow, for example) causes a physical reaction of one sort or another, whether it be an increased pulse and breathing rate triggered by adrenaline or a feeling of malaise brought on by hormones or ". . . newly discovered brain substances, endorphins and enkephalins, and activities of the nervous pathways that mediate and alter the stress response."*

Dr. Selye puts the situation this way. "They (the events) produce a body change—in effect, a derangement. And, having done so, they also make a demand on the body to readjust itself. This demand is nonspecific. It requires adaptation to a problem regardless of what the problem may be.

"That is to say that all agents [heat, cold, jogging, drugs, hormones] to which we are exposed produce not only their specific actions but also a nonspecific increase in the need to perform certain adaptive functions and then to reestablish normalcy—and the nonspecific is independent of the specific activity that caused the rise in requirements. This nonspecific demand for activity as such is the essence of stress.

"It doesn't matter whether the agent or situation we face is pleasant or unpleasant. All that counts—from the standpoint of stress-producing, or stressor, activity—is the intensity of the demand for readjustment or adaptation.

* Hans Selye, "On Executive Stress," *Executive Health,* October, 1981, p. 2.

"If it seems difficult to see how such different things as heat, cold, drugs, sorrow, and joy can provoke an identical biochemical reaction, nevertheless it can be demonstrated by actual quantitative biochemical measurements that certain reactions of the body are totally nonspecific and common to all types of exposure.

"Stress is not something to be avoided; in fact, it cannot be avoided. As the response to a stressor, a stimulus, a set of circumstances that induces a change in the flow of physiological and/or psychological functioning, it's inevitable and as essential and useful a part of living as changes in breathing and blood circulation produced when exercise is the stressor.

"Depending upon their intensity and the way they affect the individual, stress reactions can be pleasurable as well as helpful. *But when they are inappropriate or excessive, they can exhaust the capacity to respond and lead to difficulty—emotional distress, behavioral disturbances, or symptoms of illness."*

Dr. Selye goes on to say that included on the list of stress-related diseases are peptic ulcers, high blood pressure, and many others.

Now what does all this mean to the entrepreneur? It means that whether the fledgling business does well or poorly, the absolute number of significant events good and bad, real and imagined, cascading down on the founders and managers is likely to be high. When the number of events is compounded by the inherent risk of failure in both an economic and a psychological sense, it is easy to understand why stress goes with the territory, particularly in the earlier stages of growth.

Physical and mental robustness is achieved, like most everything else in life, through conscious effort. The components of such an effort seem to boil down to this list:

---

* Ibid., p.2.

- Exercise, food and drink in amounts that result in a physical condition which has a high degree of resilience.
- Purposefulness in one's *chosen* work.
- Avocational interests that regularly require undivided attention.
- Perspective on the risks and rewards of decision making which is a major component of your professional lifestyle as an entrepreneur.
- Simplicity, even in the face of gargantuan success.

Detailed consideration of these components is beyond the scope of this book. But research indicates that the more the matter of physical and mental health in executives is studied, the more these five tend to stand out as signposts along the road to a full life. Since stress itself is a biochemical phenomenon, you need to keep your body well tuned, resilient. Purposefulness is the flip (and positive) side of uselessness and its byproduct, frustration. A serious avocation is useful like a haircut. You enjoy or at least endure a short respite and come away different—at least temporarily. Decisions are the tracks that change runs on, but you can't cover much distance without encountering some ups, downs, and twists along the way. Planning helps you select the optimum routing. And simplicity, from cars and clothes to food and entertainment, is one of the few proactive defenses against the turbulence of these fast-paced times.

A wise person once said, "A man is rich who has enough." Enough for the effective entrepreneur is more than just a shot at millionairedom. There are more passive ways to accumulate a large net worth. Entrepreneuring is really a lifestyle choice, but it has its dangers. A new enterprise, being small, fragile, and even beguiling, can be loved to death, especially by its parents. Excessive affection and the intertwining of personalities with the sinews of the business may be acceptable practices for the permanently small businesses of the world, but they have limited application in a high growth, business-building situation.

Does the above point of view preclude wide-eyed enthusiasm and the do-or-die attitudes generally attributed to successful entrepreneurs and always espoused by them in speeches *after* they have emerged into the limelight? Of course not. The best analogy is that of a sports hero or heroine. While the contest is on, there is no limit to what the leader will pour into the pursuit of victory. And he or she will exhort his or her teammates to excel at almost any cost. But when the contest is over, the hero or heroine who lost doesn't despair for long or drink himself or herself into a stupor. He or she accepts what happened, tries to learn from it, goes on living, and aims to win next time. That's professionalism, the kind of professionalism that is a growing part of entrepreneuring in these increasingly complex times.

Seeing Around Corners

▼

THE TENTH COMMANDMENT

ANTICIPATE INCESSANT CHANGE BY PERIODICALLY TESTING ADOPTED BUSINESS PLANS FOR THEIR CONSISTENCY WITH THE REALITIES OF THE WORLD MARKETPLACE.

The past will not come again. Neither isolation nor insulation from tomorrow is possible. The problems of the times are the opportunities of the times, as always, but the strings attached are multiplying. Governments and new competitors, domestic and foreign, will increasingly affect the conduct of a business. So will social evolution. Despair has little value. Vigilance is required.

There's no room for entrepreneuring in a static society. So Commandment Ten carries good news. We are in the midst of a lot of change; the year 2010 is closer to us than 1980; the world has shrunk and is increasingly wired together; and today is the first day of the rest of your life. The cliches abound. But the average person is swept along by events, turning his or her head from side to side occasionally as birthdays flash by. Then the day arrives when the energy required to deviate from the worn path exceeds the energy remaining in the reservoir, and what might have been will never be. Commandment Ten is an admonishment: Take advantage of the turbulence to build something new. Commandment Ten is a warning: Systematically tune what you are building to the times.

Graphically, the challenges of the times can be depicted this way using the same Stages of Growth model used in Commandment Nine.

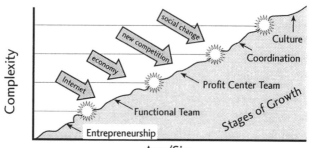

Challanges of the Times in Entrepreneuring

Entrepreneur/managers of growth companies must contend with two kinds of pressures, those from within and those from without. From within, both increasing size and complexity generate various problems and crises. They were outlined in Commandment Nine. From without, as depicted by the fat arrows, an increasing number of pressures affect a growing company as it becomes more and more viable and visible. The overriding question for the leaders of a dynamic enterprise is quite simple: What do we do to keep on succeeding? The name of the game keeps changing! There are six specific actions implicit in the dictates of the Tenth Commandment:

- Recognize and deal with reality.
- Adjust your managing style to fit the changing needs of the enterprise.
- Treat organizational structure as a variable.
- Nurture a *process* of managing within the company.
- Verbalize information and expectations.
- Remain doggedly customer centered.

These are the actions required to anticipate incessant change in order to amend your plans for the business accordingly.

Recognize and deal with reality. Floating interest and exchange rates are a reality. Diversity in the work force at all levels of responsibility is a reality. The merging of communications and computing and information delivery methods is a reality. Varied new competition in virtually any kind of growth industry is a reality. Privatization in many countries around the world is a reality. The list goes on. Some of the factors may be pivotal to your company. You must determine which ones they are and weave them into your thinking.

CASE V. Throughout the 1980s one of the major, worldwide accounting and auditing firms had a large-scale planning meeting every year. The forty-to-sixty top people in the firm attended. Early in each meeting the senior managing part-

(case continued on next page)

ner would recount progress since the last meeting. The lines on all his multicolored charts swept gracefully upwards and to the right as the decade moved along. The firm was getting progressively larger in terms of total billings; profitability was keeping pace with billings; and per-partner income stair stepped up quite nicely, year to year. There was some concern that the number of clients in the client base was shrinking slightly over time, but little urgency was attached to the matter in light of all the good news.

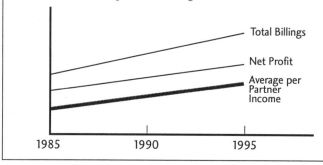

In 1990, the senior managing partner of the firm and his two key associates took a look at the past decade of the firm in constant dollars, that is, with figures adjusted for inflation. Had the trio been a little younger, the findings might have "blown their minds." As it was, they experienced a profound sense of shock. Instead of growing, the firm had actually been shrinking over the previous ten years. In real terms, the chart looked like this:

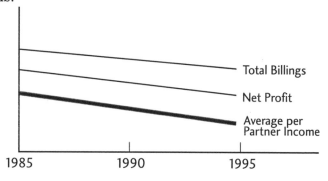

When the drop in total fees, profits, and per-partner income was added to the shrinking client base, it was clear that the firm, in total, had stopped succeeding. The reality was that the firm was starting to fail.

Most competent management teams can respond to reality if they know what it is, but it's easy to see and hear only what's comfortable in the rush of day-to-day events. And subordinates, as a rule, shy away from being harbingers of potentially noxious tidings. One of the most practical safeguards a team of entrepreneurs can have is a board of directors or advisors that is qualified and doesn't hesitate to inject hard questions and objectivity into the enterprise. Two other safeguards are a proper managing process that forces news, good and bad, to the surface and regular senior-level contacts with customers.

Adjust your managing style to fit the changing needs of the enterprise. Any entrepreneur with industrial experience is familiar with the pluses of the "-tions" in a business: communication, instruction, delegation, motivation, and recognition. These -tions don't just happen. Someone at the top causes them to happen, usually both by example and by direction. The ideal case is when these -tion elements of achieving results through others are an acquired taste bred into the fabric of the enterprise from the start so there is an ever-growing core of talent available to respond to the times. The alternative to breeding is on-the-job training or, sometimes, a crash program of management development triggered by some emergency.

CASE W. The management of a relatively young, medium-size bank holding company with an excellent record of growth and performance found itself between a rock and a hard place in the mid-1980s. The reality of banking was one of deregulation, consolidation in the industry, massive

(case continued on next page)

new competition, and tidelike costs of money, the bank's primary product. There seemed to be three ways to survive the onslaught of change. One was to expand via acquisition, that is, to buy up smaller banks in the state in order to move above the medium-size range and become less vulnerable to takeover. A second course of action was to diversify into more nonbanking activities where there appeared to be firmer ground. The third course was to tighten down on expenses and drive short-term performance upward as a prelude to selling the entire holding company to one of several suitors who had made overtures.

The third alternative was thought by management to be the least desirable. Upon analysis, however, it was the only viable one simply because the company did not have the necessary talent and systems to manage either a lot more banks or nonbanking activities. "The well is near dry," is the way the CEO put the situation. There was sadness in his voice.

Any individual's managing style is composed of numerous components, and it is clear that not every one of them has to be adjusted continuously. For entrepreneurs, the biggest single challenge is usually to let go of responsibility *and* authority as the venture ripens into an ongoing business. Delegating is the operational word. Delegating is not a skill as much as it is an attitude. When you push responsibility outwards and downwards, you do give up something . . . particularly some chances to be *a* or *the* star. But you and the enterprise also gain eyes, ears, arms, legs, and minds that will grow stronger and sharper with encouragement over time. A growth business is a team effort–more analogous to professional football or basketball than to golf. Effective teams have good coaches or player/coaches who can change roles with alacrity.

Treat organization structure as a variable. The typical progression in most companies is to move over time from a functional organization structure to a profit center structure, as outlined in Commandment Nine.

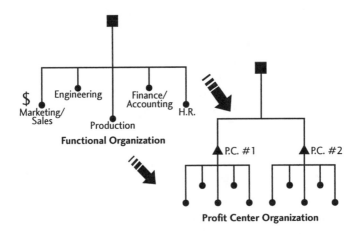

Functional Organization

$ Marketing/ Sales   Engineering   Production   Finance/ Accounting   H.R.

Profit Center Organization

P.C. #1   P.C. #2

This general progression tends to make sense as the use of profit centers breaks the enterprise up into smaller pieces, develops more general managers, etc. It is important to recognize that there are countless variations and permutations along the way having to do with position titles, reporting relationships, salary brackets, and all the administrative paraphernalia that goes with facilitating a group of humans working together. Ideally, the culture of the company will highly value flexibility, cooperation, and appropriate competitiveness. At a minimum, entrepreneurs will do well to downplay from the start the significance of the classic status symbols of corporate life that can make for premature hardening of the business arteries, i.e. structural rigidity in the face of internal and external change.

CASE X. From day one, the four cofounders of a biomed company decided that they would share the decisions and power in the company. This philosophy has permeated the organization which today employs more than 100 people, many of them skilled technologists and scientists. Ramifications of the philosophy include a total absence of private offices and private secretaries, no titles on business cards, group reviews of peer performance, rotating committee chairpersonships, and only a few broad job classifications for salary administration purposes. To date, after fifteen months, the company has met or exceeded all its milestones and projections.

Whether the management of Case X can make its philosophy work when it has 500 employees is still an open question. But there is evidence that, so far, little energy is being burned with internecine struggles for attention and recognition. And the company is proving to be very adaptable to the unfolding mix of customer and distribution-system requirements being placed on it. This is an extreme case, but structure in its broadest sense has truly been treated as a variable during company X's formative period.

Nurture a process of managing within the company. The key word is *process*. It implies a continuing, consistent, if not repetitive, sequence of events over time during which the participants can get to know one another, come to share a common vision and vocabulary, and establish a sense of order in the life of the enterprise. There are enough surprises in the day-to-day existence of a young company. Irregularities and spontaneity in the way managers conduct themselves are superfluous, if not downright destructive.

CASE Y. A high-flying electronic game company went bankrupt after the heart of its programming and engineering staff walked out and set up shop down the street. Among the deficiencies articulated by the departees were the following:

Ad hoc salary adjustments (increases)...usually only when a person threatened to leave.

No information on company plans (and doubts as to whether any plans actually existed).

No feedback on either company or personal performance.

Lack of confidence in the competence of two of the three top executives. ("They didn't seem to know what they were doing.")

Continuous fire drills in terms of who was to do what, by when ("Perpetual panic").

In sum, the management function (as contrasted to the programming and engineering functions) of the company was bush league in comparison to the very large market opportunity confronting the enterprise. What started out as a venture turned into an adventure rather than a business. The original entrepreneurs lost out.

Where does a process originate? As a practical matter, the written business plan can usefully serve as the centerpiece around which a discrete managing process is formulated. An updated business plan is needed for each coming year. Picture a management team that meets a half day per month solely to review progress and think ahead. Here are the kinds of subjects that could form the skeleton of an annual process:

January   Review actual results against previous year's plan. Agree on strong and weak points. Identify business planning process changes needed.

February   Review performance of key individuals in company. Consider all compensation matters.

March   Identify major market trends and discuss implications. Analyze relations with key customers.

April   Agree upon an economic forecast for the coming twelve months and its probable impact on operations. Crystallize any required action. Write down assumptions.

May   Establish a planning timetable and methodology for the coming year's business plan. Consider what's new in planning techniques.

June   Discuss trends in technology that can affect any phase of the business. Assign "watchers" or resource people to keep current on specific items of interest.

July   Review six-month results against annual plan. Note any weaknesses in assumptions. Make necessary revisions for second half.

August   Set corporate and planning unit objectives for coming year.

September   Listen to and discuss plans proposed by planning unit leaders. (Planning unit leaders may be profit-center managers, functional vice-presidents, product managers, etc.)

October   Same as September. Consolidate plans.

November   Review financial and human resource implications and requirements of the consolidated plan for the company. Present plan to board for comments.

December   Adopt business plan (including budgets) for coming year.

This list of subjects is not meant to be exhaustive, merely representative. And a management team that develops *and sticks to* such a calendar tailored to its own enterprise and people will have gone a long way toward establishing a process that can bring stability, insight, internal consistency, and smarter decisions to the challenges of the times. Of course the above calendar does not preclude the other meetings—planned and ad hoc—that will go on out of necessity. In fact, the existence of a senior calendar can make the interim meetings on more operational matters more efficient because the tendency to jumble short- and longer-range issues together may well be reduced.

Verbalize information and expectations. Everybody is in favor of better communication, but what does it mean? Open offices or an open-door policy? Company newsletters? Friday night beer parties for the staff? Casual, mixed-level lunches? A formal mentor system? These are all candidates for inclusion, but the heart of communicating has to do with transmitting and sharing ideas, opinions, and critiques on the work being done, the heartbeat of the company. The rest, from newsletters to parties, is just icing on the cake for a company on the move. In the final analysis, productive communicating boils down to regular boss-subordinate interchanges about the tasks at hand and those upcoming. And the value of the interchange is amplified if both parties have at least a rough understanding of what the company is all about—the vision, mission, and objectives.

Participation is an overused word with many connotations. But actual day-to-day participation in mainstream events is one of the attractions smaller companies offer to people. Yet it is often hard to retain that hands-on flavor as a company grows. It is hard to retain because the distance expands between the decision-makers (customers, founders, officers) and the average employee. It is also hard to retain because a lot of "nonjobs" get created and perpetuated. The epidemic of downsizing in established companies of late has been an attempt, in part, to solve the nonjob problem. But the former problem, distance, lingers on. There is no real solution to it other than for managers to be aggressive in helping their people succeed in their vocations. As spelled out in Commandment Six, people do indeed respond to structured expectations. And no matter how the fact may be smothered in analysis and theory, *a person's boss is his or her primary reference point in the world of work.* If that primary point is weak or vacillating, the message comes through. If that point of reference is ignorant of and noncommunicative on the health and outlook for the enterprise, how is the average employee to be adaptive, enthusiastic, and innovative?

CASE Z. AH&B, a consulting firm, grew rapidly in billings to over $6 million per year. The three founders were able to attract a lot of new talent into the company and, thereby, free-up their own time for sales work–the pursuit of new contracts. A giant opportunity in Saudi Arabia captured their imagination. It was an opportunity to design a complete new city from scratch. The three became enraptured with the project and poured many man-months and dollars into the preparation of an extensive proposal. They flew back and forth to the Mideast, waltzed the Saudi diplomats in Washington, D.C., and generally ignored the rest of the activities in their firm. They were oblivious to the resentment that slowly built up among many of the newer recruits who had been charmed aboard personally by one or more of the founders. The proposal was duly submitted in Saudi Arabia with appropriate fanfare. The date for a decision on the successful bidder came and went. Everybody waited. Then they waited some more. Months passed. The momentum of the firm slowed as first one and then other talented people left, often taking existing clients with them in the process. The AH&B founders woke up one morning to find they had lost the Saudi bid, that they had only a shell of a firm left in terms of talent still aboard, and that their two largest domestic clients of long standing had switched . . . to former employees of AH&B.

Good people don't need to stay on in the dark, and entrepreneuring can be contagious.

Remain doggedly customer-centered. Amid all the external pressures, the ones most important to respond to are those that have an impact on your customers. More than one group of entrepreneurs have been surprised to find that interest rates or foreign competition or a new technological development has suddenly put a big dent in their growth plans. Often the surprise would have been avoided if one or more of the top people had not pushed eyeball-to-eyeball customer contact down low on his or her list of things to do. For example, a year after the Saudi Arabia debacle in Case Z above, AH&B management received another blow. High interest rates drove AH&B's remaining largest client, a highly leveraged, second-home developer, into bankruptcy. This demise could have been foreseen by an alert observer of the client and the times, and someone at AH&B should have been that alert observer.

How does a new venture get and stay customer oriented? The signals have to come firmly and regularly from the top. The burden is on the entrepreneur.

Commandment Ten calls on the entrepreneur to keep on entrepreneuring in the sense of monitoring and responding accurately to ever-changing reality. Doing this is central to serving society in some useful way on a continuing basis...central to keeping on succeeding. In recent years, IBM, Westinghouse, RCA, US Air, Wang, and many other business icons have fallen from grace. Some years ago *Business Week* published a study of thirty-seven Fortune 500 companies whose managements are generally considered to have been effective in extending the youthful spirit of their enterprises over many, many years, through good times and bad.* The study indicated that the managements of these companies shared eight attributes:

* Thomas J. Peters, "Putting Excellence into Management," *Business Week,* July 21, 1980, pp. 196-205.

A bias toward action
Simple form and lean staff
Continued contact with customers
Productivity improvement via people
Operational autonomy
Stress on one key business value
Emphasis on doing what they know best
Simultaneous loose/tight controls

These attributes have their roots in entrepreneuring. They highlight the central tenet of this book which is that entrepreneuring is the Olympics of capitalism. The hard work and sacrifices may be great, but the satisfactions are great, too, for those who choose to participate.

Steve Brandt

Introduction to the Appendices

After completing an effective, practical book, an inspired reader is often faced with the dilemma: Now that I know all this, what do I do first? This very natural question is particularly tough to answer for a would-be entrepreneur because he or she is potentially faced with some monumental tasks if dreams are going to be converted to reality. Do you, entrepreneurial reader, at this moment have a business concept? Is there a market opportunity upon which your concept can feed and flourish? Have you identified the precise kinds of people and how much money you will need to translate the concept into concrete? Have you moved your findings and thinking out of your head and onto paper in a reasonably orderly fashion to see if they can withstand hard scrutiny by knowledgeable folks whose opinions you respect? These are the big league questions generally required to systematically get a new growth company properly launched.

Three appendices follow to help existing and would-be entrepreneurs bridge the gap between the Ten Commandments and managing their own going concerns.

Appendix A is a short guide to analyzing an industry or market. It was developed originally by Michael Porter of the Harvard Business School for use by students in various courses, including courses having to do with small business development. Nailing down the magnitude of the market opportunity in quantitative terms is a chore many entrepreneurs would happily forego. It's much easier to deal with soft facts. Every entrepreneur "knows" the market is out there. Why bother researching it? And once in a while a shot in the dark does pay off. Once in a while. Appendix A is included as a supplement to both Commandments Two and Four to help you double your probability to "twice in a while."

Appendix B provides a simple table of contents for a business plan. It is important for an entrepreneur to cover the bases, i.e., make sure that he or she has adequately thought about the subjects listed. Substance is more important than form, but don't underestimate the importance of how a finished business plan looks if you are submitting it to professional investors for evaluation.

Appendix C is an actual business plan. Over the years your author has dealt with several hundred business plans of all shapes and sizes. He has had many requests for a sample plan. Appendix C is one such plan. The Cdex Corporation plan is not included as a model, but rather as a somewhat abbreviated sample. It has both strengths and weaknesses, promise and problems. You are encouraged to read it critically and to jot down your reactions. Then answer this question for yourself: Did the management team of Cdex significantly increase their chances for business success by getting their thinking down on paper and exposing it to outside review enroute to starting Cdex for real?

Appendix A
*How to Conduct an Industry Analysis**

How should one go about analyzing an industry and competitors? What types of data does one look for and how can they be organized? Where does one look for these data? This appendix deals with these questions and some of the other practical problems involved in conducting an industry analysis. There are basically two types of data about industries: published data and those gathered from interviews with industry participants and observers (field data). The bulk of discussion in this appendix will center on identifying the important sources of published and field data, their strengths and weaknesses, and strategies for approaching them most effectively and in the right sequence.

A full-blown industry analysis is a massive task, and one that can consume months if one is starting from scratch. In beginning an industry analysis there is a tendency to dive in and collect a mass of detailed information, with little in the way of a general framework or approach in which to fit this information. This lack of method leads to frustration at best, and confusion and wasted effort at worst. Thus before considering specific sources, it is important to consider an overall strategy for conducting the industry study and the critical first steps in initiating it.

INDUSTRY ANALYSIS STRATEGY

There are two important aspects in developing a strategy for analyzing an industry. The first is to determine just what it is one is looking for. "Anything about the industry" is much too broad to serve as an effective guide for research. Although the full list of specific issues that need to be addressed in an industry analysis depends on the particular industry under study, it is possible to generalize about what important information and raw data the researcher should look for. Key structural features, important forces causing them to change, and

---

*Reprinted with permission of Macmillan Publishing Co., Inc., from *Competitive Strategy* by Michael Porter. Copyright © 1980 by The Free Press.

strategic information on competitors are basic areas of inquiry. These are factors that are the target of an industry analysis. However, since these characteristics of structure and competitors are generally not raw data but rather the result *of analysis* of raw data, researchers may also find it useful to have a framework for systematically collecting raw data. A simple but exhaustive set of areas under which to collect raw data is given in Figure A-1.

Figure A-1.
Raw Data Categories for Industry Analysis

Data Categories	*Compilation*
Product lines	By company
Buyers and their behavior	By year
Complementary products	By functional area
Substitute products	
Growth Rate	
Pattern (seasonal, cyclical)	
Determinants	
Technology of production and distribution	
Cost structure	
Economies of scale	
Value added	
Logistics	
Labor	
Marketing and Selling	
Market segmentation	
Marketing practices	
Suppliers	
Distribution channels (if indirect)	
Innovation	
Types	
Sources, Rate of	
Economies of scale	
Competitors-strategy, goals, strengths and weaknesses, assumptions	
Social, political, legal environment	
Macroeconomic environment	

The researcher who can fully describe each of these areas should be in a position to develop a comprehensive picture of industry structure and competitors' profiles.

With a framework for assembling data, the second major strategy question is how sequentially to develop data in each area. There are a number of alternatives, ranging from taking one item at a time to proceeding randomly. However, there are important benefits in getting a general *overview* of the industry first, and only then focusing on the specifics. Experience has shown that a broad understanding can help the researcher more effectively spot important items of data when studying sources and organize data more effectively as they are collected.

A number of steps can be useful in obtaining this overview:

1. Who is in the industry. It is wise to develop a rough list of industry participants right away, especially the leading firms. A list of key competitors is helpful for quickly finding other articles and company documents (some of the sources discussed later will aid in this process). An entering wedge for many of these sources is the industry's *Standard Industrial Classification* (SIC) code, which can be determined from the Census Bureau's *Standard Industrial Classification Manual.* The SIC system classifies industries on a variety of levels of breadth, with two-digit industries overly broad for most purposes, five-digit industries often too narrow, and four-digit industries usually about right.

2. Industry studies. If one is lucky, there may be a relatively comprehensive industry study available or a number of broadly-based articles. Reading these can be a quick way of developing an overview. (Sources of industry studies are discussed later.)

3. Annual reports. If there are any publicly held firms in the industry, annual reports should be consulted early. A single annual report may contain only modest amounts of disclosure. However, a quick review of the annual reports for a number of major companies over a ten- or fifteen-year period is an excellent way to begin to understand the industry. Most aspects of the business will be discussed at one time or another. The most enlightening part of an annual report for an overview is often the president's letter. The researcher should look for the rationales given for both good and bad financial results; these should expose some of the critical success factors in the industry. It also is important to note what the company seems to be proud of in its annual report, what it seems to be worried about, and what key changes have been made. It is also possible to gain some insights into how companies are organized, the flow of production, and numerous other factors from reading between the lines in a series of annual reports from the same company.

The researcher will generally want to come back to annual reports and other company documents later in the study. The initial early reading will fail to uncover many nuances that become apparent once the knowledge of the industry and the competitor is more complete.

Get into the field early. If there is any common problem in getting industry analyses underway, it is that researchers tend to spend too much time looking for published sources and using the library before they begin to tap field sources. Published sources have a variety of limitations: timeliness, level of aggregation, depth, and so on. Although it is important to gain some basic understanding of the industry to maximize the value of field interviews, the researcher should not exhaust all published sources *before* getting into the field. On the contrary, clinical and library research should proceed simultaneously. They tend to feed on each other, especially if the researcher is aggressive in asking every field source to suggest published material about the industry. Field sources tend to be more efficient because they get to the issues, without the wasted time of reading useless documents. Interviews also sometimes help the researcher identify the issues. This help may come, to some extent, at the expense of objectivity.

Get over the hump. Experience shows that the morale of researchers in an industry study often goes through a U-shaped cycle as the study proceeds. An initial period of euphoria gives way to confusion and even panic as the complexity of the industry becomes apparent and mounds of information accumulate. Sometime later in the study, it all begins to come together. This pattern appears to be so common as to serve as a useful thing for researchers to remember.

The amount of published information available varies widely by industry. The larger the industry, the older it is, and the slower the rate of technological change, the better the available published information tends to be. Unfortunately for the researcher, many interesting industries do not meet these criteria, and there may be little published information available. However, it is *always* possible to gain some important information about an industry from published sources, and these sources should be aggressively pursued. Generally, the problem the researcher will face in using published data for analyzing an economically meaningful industry is that they are *too broad,* or too aggregated, to fit the industry. If a researcher starts searching for data with this reality in mind, the usefulness of broad data will be better recognized and the tendency to give up too easily will be avoided.

Two important principles can greatly facilitate the development of references to published materials. First, every published source should be combed tenaciously for references to other sources, both other published sources and sources for field interviews. Often articles will cite individuals (industry executives, security analysts, and so on) who usually do not appear by accident; they tend to be either well-informed or particularly vocal industry observers, and they make excellent leads.

The second principle is to keep a thorough bibliography of everything that is uncovered. Although it is painful at the time, taking down the full citation of the source not only saves time in compiling the bibliography at the end of the study but also guards against wasteful duplication of efforts by members of research teams and the agony of not being able to remember where some critical piece of information came from. Summary notes on sources or copies are also useful. They minimize the need for rereading and can facilitate communication within a research team.

Although the types of published sources are potentially numerous, they can be divided into a number of general categories, which are discussed briefly below.

Industry studies. Studies that provide a general overview of some industries come in two general varieties. First are book-length studies of the industry, often (but not exclusively) written by economists. These can usually best be found in library card catalogs and by cross-checking references given in other sources. Participants in or observers of an industry will almost always know of such industry studies when they exist, and they should be questioned about them as the study proceeds.

The second broad category is the typically shorter, more focused studies conducted by securities or consulting firms, such as Frost and Sullivan, Arthur D. Little, SRI and all the Wall Street research houses. Sometimes specialized consulting firms collect data on particular industries, such as SMART, Inc., in the ski industry and IDC in the computer industry. Often access to these studies involves a fee. Unfortunately, although there are a number of published directories of market research studies, there is no one place where they are all compiled, and the best way to learn about them is through industry observers or participants.

Trade associations. Many industries have trade associations, which serve as clearing houses for industry data and sometimes publish detailed industry statistics. Trade associations differ greatly in their willingness to give data to researchers. Usually, however, an introduction from a member of the association is helpful in gaining the cooperation of staff in sending data.

Whether or not the association is a source of data, members of the staff are extremely useful in alerting the researcher to any published information about the industry that exists, identifying the key participants and discussing their general impressions of how the industry functions, its key factors for company success, and important industry trends. Once contact with a trade association staff member has been made, this person can in turn be a useful source of referrals to industry participants and can identify participants who represent a range of viewpoints.

Trade magazines. Most industries have one or more trade magaines which cover industry events on a regular (sometimes even daily) basis. A small industry may be covered as part of a broader-based trade publication. Trade journals in customer, distributor, or supplier industries are often useful sources as well.

Reading through trade magazines over a long period of time is an extremely useful way to understand the competitive dynamics and important changes in an industry, as well as to diagnose its norms and attitudes.

Business press. A wide variety of business publications cover companies and industries on an intermittent basis. To obtain references, there are a number of standard bibliographies, including the *Business Periodicals Index, The Wall Street Journal Index,* and the *F&S Index,* United States (and companions for Europe and International).

Company directories and statistical data. There are a variety of directories of both public and private U.S. firms, some of which give a limited amount of data. Many directories list firms by SIC code, and thus they provide a way to build a complete list of industry participants. Comprehensive directories include *Thomas Register of American Manufacturers,* the Dun and Bradstreet *Million Dollar Directory and Middle Market Directory, Standard and Poor's Register of Corporations, Directors and Executives,* and the various *Moody's* publications. Another broad list of companies classified by industry is the Newsfront 30,000 *Leading U.S. Corporations,* which gives some limited financial information as well. In addition to these general directories, other potential sources of broad company lists are financial magazines *(Fortune, Forbes)* and buyers guides.

Dun and Bradstreet compiles credit reports on all companies of significant size, whether they be public or private. These reports are not available in any library and are provided only to subscribing companies who pay a high fixed cost for the service plus a small fee for individual reports. Dun and Bradstreet reports are valuable as sources about private companies, but since data provided by the companies are not audited, it must be used with caution; many users have reported errors in the information.

There are also many statistical sources of data such as advertising spending and stock market performance.

Company documents. Most companies publish a variety of documents about themselves, particularly if they are publicly traded. In addition to annual reports, SEC Form 10 K's, proxy statements, prospectuses, and other government filings can be useful. Also useful are speeches or testimony by firm executives, press releases, product literature, manuals, published company histories, transcripts of annual meetings, want ads, patents, and even advertising.

Major government sources. The Internal Revenue Service provides in the *IRS Corporation Source Book of Statistics of Income* extensive annual financial information on industries (by size of organizations within the industry) based on corporate tax returns. A less detailed, printed version of the data is in the IRS's *Statistics of Income.* The main drawback of this source is that the financial data for an entire company are allocated to that company's principle industry, thereby introducing biases in industries in which many participants are highly diversified. However, the IRS data are available annually back to the 1940s, and it is the only source that gives financial data covering all firms in the industry.

Another source of government statistics is the Bureau of the Census. The most frequently used volumes are *Census of Manufacturers, Census of Retail Trade, and Census of the Mineral Industries,* which are available quite far back in time. As with the IRS data, the census does not refer to specific companies but rather breaks down statistics by SIC code. Census material also has considerable regional data for industries. Unlike IRS data, census data are based on aggregates of data from establishments within corporations, such as plant sites and warehouses, rather than corporations as a whole. Therefore, the data are not biased by company diversification. One feature of the *Census of Manufacturers* that can be particularly useful is the special report, *Concentration Ratios in Manufacturing Industry.* This section gives the percentages of industry sales of the largest four, eight, twenty, and fifty firms in the industry for each SIC four-digit manufacturing industry in the economy. Another useful government source for price level changes in industries is the Bureau of Labor Statistics, *Wholesale Price Index.*

Leads on further government information can be obtained through the various indexes of government publications, as well as by contacting the U.S. Department of Commerce and the libraries of other government agencies. Other government sources include regulatory agency filings, congressional hearings, and patent office statistics.

Other sources. Some other potentially fruitful published sources include the following:
- antitrust records;
- local newspapers in which a competitor's facilities or headquarters are located;
- local tax records.

As indicated earlier, published data compliments field data, and vice-versa.

Appendix B

Guide to Preparing a Business Plan*

TABLE OF CONTENTS

*See Commandment Four, p. 37

4.5 Program for initial time period
4.6 Schedule–who is to do what, by when (Exhibit)
4.7 Budget (Exhibit)
4.8 Results expected (Exhibit)
4.9 Contingency plans

Section 5.0 Marketing
5.1 Method(s) of selling and advertising to be employed
5.2 Product or service features and benefits to be emphasized
5.3 Program for initial time period
5.4 Schedule–who is to do what, by when (Exhibit)
5.5 Budget (Exhibit)
5.6 Results expected (Exhibit)
5.7 Contingency plans

Section 6.0 Organization & People
6.1 Who is accountable to whom, for what. Organizational Design (Exhibit)
6.2 Staffing program for initial time period
6.3 Schedule (Exhibit)
6.4 Budget (Exhibit)
6.5 Results expected (e.g. brief position descriptions)
6.6 Contingency plans

Section 7.0 Funds Flow & Financial Projections
7.1 Projected cash flows from operations, i.e. total funds in and out for the initial time period (Exhibit)
7.2 Proforma profit and loss statements (Exhibit)
7.3 Proforma balance sheets (Exhibit)
7.4 Program for monitoring and controlling funds, people and systems

Section 8.0 Ownership
     8.1 Summary of funding requirements
     8.2 Form of business–partnership, corporation, etc.
     8.3 Program for raising equity and/or debt money required, if any
     8.4 Projected returns to investors (Exhibit)

Note: If technology is an important ingredient in the success of the enterprise, a separate section, Technology, should probably be included in the Business Plan. Such a section would include details on staffing and methods of inquiry and testing as well as schedules, budgets, results expected, and contingency plans.

Appendix C

Sample Business Plan

The following is an actual business plan that was submitted by the management of Cdex Corporation to ten different, practicing venture capitalists in an attempt to raise the $500,000 needed to carry out the plan. The plan included here is essentially complete. Only a few financial details that were in the actual plan have been omitted. In addition, personal and company names have been changed in some cases to protect the parties involved.

You are urged to read the plan carefully. Assume or pretend you are a potential investor or key employee. What is your evaluation of the plan? Does it seem to be consistent with the Ten Commandmentsparticularly number four, Preparing a Business Plan? What weaknesses and strengths strike you as you read the plan? What questions would you ask the Cdex management in a face-to-face interview? Would you be inclined to invest, given sound answers from the management?

Make note of your comments and reactions on the next page as you read the plan. Then compare your thoughts to those of the ten venture capitalists who actually reviewed the plan. Their comments are shown in the Epilogue to this Appendix C.

AN EVALUATION OF THE CDEX CORPORATION BUSINESS PLAN

SECTION	STRENGTHS	WEAKNESSES	QUESTIONS/ COMMENTS
1.0 Concept			
2.0 Objectives			
3.0 Market Analysis			
4.0 Production			
5.0 Marketing			
6.0 Organization & People			
7.0 Funds Flow & Financial Projections			
8.0 Ownership			

Preface

The accompanying projections reflect Cdex Corporation management's best current estimate of future operating results. All the figures shown are based upon currently available information and certain management assumptions. Because these projections depend in part upon future events, some of which may be beyond management's control, no assurance can be given that the projections will be achieved.

Cdex Corporation
Business Plan
January 19XX

EXECUTIVE SUMMARY

Over the next twenty years, technology in the form of microcomputers is expected by the founders and management of Cdex to revolutionize the process of training and developing corporate employees. Currently microcomputers are being purchased by businesses and professional people for use on accounting-type applications. Cdex management expects the market for nonaccounting applications of the microcomputer to grow rapidly in the years ahead. Further, Cdex expects to be a leader in providing nonaccounting-type programs. In short, Cdex is aiming to be the first electronic publisher of human resources development materials.

During 19XX four pilot programs were developed, produced, and demonstrated to a variety of potential buyers. In addition, marketing and staffing matters were thrashed out and resolved. The business plan that follows reflects the 19XX work. Management now wishes to raise $500,000 from private investors to take advantage of the opportunity explained in the plan.

I. CONCEPT

Cdex will become the premier electronic publisher of materials for selected market segments in the United States and abroad. Electronic publishing best describes what our company will do; management development material on disks that run on personal computers best describes the nature of our product during our early years. Record publishers sell music on CD's and tapes to which customers listen after inserting the medium into the appropriate machine; book publishers sell information and entertainment on printed and bound pieces of paper which individual customers read at their own pace; Cdex will sell information and performance improvement on floppy disks which corporations and individuals will buy and use in conjunction with personal computers. People taking Cdex programs will personally become more effective and more efficient in their work. Cdex will become an important force in improving "white collar" productivity.

In time, Cdex will have a large library of programs written by a cross section of recognized experts on a variety of subjects vital to the chosen market segments. In the early years, we will concentrate on accepted management development subjects for which there are already proven commercial markets including supervisory training, profit planning, selling skills, managing by objectives, and problem solving. A complete list of the initial forty programs currently under development is included in Exhibit 1, the maiden Cdex information brochure.

The Cdex management team and board feel, based on experience, that there are five major ingredients required if Cdex is to capitalize on the opportunity being spawned by the well-documented microcomputer boom:

1. Proven subjects (titles) to sell
2. Material in a superior format and medium—superior from the individual users' points of view
3. Dependable delivery systems (microcomputers)
4. Smart marketing, particularly with regards to distribution
5. Sufficient financing to achieve a critical mass of material and market recognition relatively quickly

When present, these five will propel Cdex into the forefront of the embryonic field of electronic publishing.

1. Proven subjects to sell. Two proofs are required for each subject selected for the Cdex library. First, there must be known commercial interest in the subject in the primary segment, the business and professional marketplace. A known commercial interest means that the subject is already commonly taught/bought for management/salesperson development uses. It may currently be bought in a book, videotape, seminar, manual, or in-house trainer format, but it must already be a popular, purchased development subject. Cdex is not interested in sellng both the need for the subject and the medium, only the medium, i.e. computer-assisted, interactive, audiovisual human resource development programs "off the shelf."

The second proof required for admittance to the Cdex library is that subject have a creditable authority/author behind it. Cdex is a publisher, not (strictly speaking) a creator of materials. We wish to take the best information already available and important to our primary segment and apply modern technology to it to enhance its digestibility, on-the-job use, and benefit-to-cost ratio. The initial programs in the Cdex library were prepared by the author of a best-selling business book, and plans are underway (see later) to expand the stable of Cdex authors starting later this year.

2. Material in a superior format and medium. Interactive, multimedia, self-pacing instruction has long been identified as a powerful *learning technology* in terms of impact, retention, and speed for teaching most (not all) adult/business subjects. This technology has been around for years, but the hardware (delivery systems) and necessary software have not. Now the hardware (microcomputers) is readily available; but a software vacuum already exists and it will mushroom in the years ahead. Cdex will puncture that vacuum and aid the revolution away from manuals, meetings (seminars), and memos...where they are not the best solution to the manager-and-people development opportunity.

Statistics commonly used to illustrate one aspect of the superiority of technology used by Cdex are those having to do with learner retention of material taught. In general, research indicates that people tend to remember roughly . . .

10 percent of what they hear
20 percent of what they see
30 percent of what they see and hear
60 percent of what they see, hear, and do (interact with)

Cdex programs take full advantage of these findings plus provide individuals with the opportunity to self pace and repeat trips through the subjects. Further, corporate users gain the key advantage of achieving *consistency* over time and across their organizations when Cdex programs form the core of the management development effort. Cdex programs are not subject to the variations in quality and content found in materials delivered live by trainers. For example, technology now makes it possible for all of a company's supervisors to get precisely the same message and retain it.

3. Dependable delivery systems. Microcomputers have come of age very rapidly. Unlike the highly fragmented, single purpose "teaching machine" boom (and bust) of the 1960s, microcomputers are catching on (40 percent growth rate per year) with business and professional people based on solid, varied applications with tangible payoffs. Much of the emphasis at this time is on financial/accounting/number crunching programs ("software"). Cdex management believes there is a substantial opportunity for nonnumber, nongame programs already, and that the company can be a leader in this part of the software program market as it expands.

All of the major microcomputer manufacturers (Apple, Compaq, IBM, HP) have extensive machine service networks supporting their multimillion-dollar marketing programs. In the 1960s, hardware was a liability for training and development applications. Today, it is definitely an asset.

4. Smart marketing, particularly with regards to distribution. Given one, two, and three above, Cdex management's marketing concept is to tackle the corporate/business/professional market simultaneously from three directions. First, we are exploring distribution agreements with major manufacturers, specifically Apple and IBM upon whose equipment Cdex programs initially run. Second, Cdex will expand its direct, corporate sales effort with the addition of senior salespeople once financing is completed. And third, the first Cdex Training Center will open in the heart of Silicon Valley (Sunnyvale, California) by mid-19XX.

We feel a multifaceted approach is desirable if Cdex is to capture the high ground of being the first successful electronic publisher of quality computer-assisted, human resource development materials.

5. Sufficient financing to achieve a critical mass of material and market recognition relatively quickly. The microcomputer revolution is bringing with it a flood of single purpose, program writers/producers. These software people are vital to the growth of the microcomputer market, and in time Cdex will publish and market certain of their works. At the same time, major traditional publishers (McGrawHill, Addison-Wesley, etc.) are busy thinking about ways they, too, can capitalize on the technological revolution, and their distribution networks are of interest to Cdex for its products. Both of the above are going on while the microcomputer manufacturers are spending money to stimulate primary demand. This all adds up to the fact that we are in the very early, confused, startup stage of a new industry.

Money ($500,000) is needed by Cdex to bring on board the small team of top people who can systematically exploit the confusion (authors, manufacturers, distribution systems, market segments) in the construction of a new kind of company, the Cdex electronic publishing company. How the money will be used and the "systematic exploitation" is covered in detail in the balance of this business plan.

II. OBJECTIVES

Overall, the Cdex management intends to build an unusually profitable $100 million company by 19XX. We are confident we can do so because a) the basic market for human resource development materials is growing rapidly and will continue to do so around the world, b) we have proprietary technology in our material preparation, and c) we expect the microcomputer revolution to provide us with delivery devices in every nook and cranny of society. In this latter regard, we will follow along behind wherever the micros are sold and used, not lead the way. More specifically, our projected profit state-

CDEX PROFIT PROJECTION 19XX–19YY

YEAR →	19XX	19XY	19XZ	19YX	19YY
# OF CU'S SOLD	39450	130500	675000	1575000	3437500
# OF DISKS SHIPPED	5000	10000	25000	50000	75000
# OF TC'S	1	2	3	5	8
# OF EMPLOYEES	22	50	100	250	400
SALES	1190850	5721525	20522250	41580000	73077000
C OF GS	119085	858229	4104450	10395000	18269250
GROSS MAR	1071765	4863296	16417800	31185000	54807750
GM% →	90	85	80	75	75
CORP DIV EXP	253258	1081160	3851760	6595320	11581040
EXP%SLS →	21	19	19	16	16
TC DIV EXP	158665	406275	752680	1273433	2046132
EXP%SLS →	13	7	4	3	3
BOTH DIV %SLS →	35	26	22	19	19
G & A	595483	949125	1081773	1519679	2086785
%SLS →	50	17	5	4	3
DEPRCN 20% CP EQ	6000	16000	36000	66000	200000
INCENTIVE COMP	0	286076	1026113	2079000	3653850
NPBT	58359	2124660	9669474	19651568	35239943
TAXES	20000	1000000	4500000	9000000	15500000
NPAT	38359	1124660	5169474	10651568	19739943
ROE	8	225	1034	—	—
ROI (CUMM CSH =1)	21	119	114	75	67
ROS	2	20	25	26	27

Legend
CU = Cdex Unit
DISK = Programs
TC = Training Centers
C OF GS = Cost of Goods Sold
CORP DIV = Corporate Div
TC DIV = Training Center Div
G&A = General and
    Administrative
DEPRCN = Depreciation
CP EQ = Capital Equipment

ments for the first five years are shown on page 164. In summary, the primary Cdex corporate objectives are as follows:

1. Achieve $100 million in sales volume by 19XX with a minimum NPBT of 25 percent.
2. Maintain an ROE exceeding 30 percent throughout the history of the company. (See balance sheets later in the business plan.)
3. Be included in the top five names mentioned in any post-19XX survey of industry-knowledgeable people who influence corporate/professional thinking on microcomputer/communications/human resource development technology.

III. MARKET ANALYSIS

The total United States market for microcomputer programs is currently considered to be in the $50-80 million class. This annual figure includes programs containing games, personal applications, and business applications. This software market is expected to grow at 40 percent per year for the foreseeable future in parallel with the microcomputer hardware market.

As mentioned earlier, the thrust of much of the new software produced in the years ahead will be toward business applications—particularly applications based on accounting information. For example, the August 19XX full-page announcements in major newspapers by both IBM and HP stressed the accounting-type applications of their "personal" computers . . . i.e., their micros. Few people/companies are prepared today to provide nonaccounting-type programs. Bell & Howell is one such company by virtue of PASS, its Professional Authoring Software System. Cdex has already licensed PASS from B&H. More on this later.

Deltak, a leading company in the training of computer people for companies, is the only known company that at this time appears to share Cdex's vision of the opportunity ahead. Deltak has historically used standup seminars and videotapes for their training programs. They, too, have become a PASS licensee, and they have recently started advertising their "Microvision" programs which run as Cdex's do—on Apple machines. Deltak is a ten-year-old, worldwide company with sales in excess of $50 million. Deltak, a venture capital funded startup, was sold recently to Prentice Hall.

In summary to this point, Cdex will sell in the wake of the obvious, accounting oriented programs which are proliferating in the marketplace. For example, we expect that most of our customers in 19XX and 19XX will already own the necessary microcomputer hardware. Over the longer run, when the market is viewed strictly in terms of microcomputer programs, Cdex expects in 19XX to be selling 5 to 10 percent of a billion dollar a year, packaged software market.

A different and more useful way to evaluate the Cdex market opportunity is to look at the money being spent on business and professional development. The American Society for Training & Development (ASTD) estimates that the total market for commercial training and development materials (seminars, books, films, posters, site costs, speakers, etc.) exceeded $1 billion in 19XX. This figure does not include the money spent for the continuing education of legal, medical, and accounting practitioners. Supervisory training packages alone (one of Cdex's major product areas) are selling at a rate of over $25 million per year through a variety of suppliers, including Louis Allen, Scientific Methods, Sterling, Kepner Tregoe, BNA, CRM, and Dartnell. Cdex is interested primarily in publishing computer-assisted materials for executives, managers, supervisors, and salespeople—the subsegments that are historically the most popular targets for packaged development materials. In 19XX, U.S. corporations are estimated to have spent well over $200 million on commercial products, seminars, and services for these four sub-segments.

While a down economy can have a dampening effect in any given year, this chosen group of four subsegments is expected to expand at an average rate of 20 percent a year without the application of microcomputer technology. Cdex management believes that its technology might add 5 percent to the natural growth rate. The end result is annual markets as shown on top of the following page.

	$Market	Cdex Share	$ Sales
19XX	200 M	1%	2.7
19XY	250	9	24.0
19XZ	310	12	37.0
19YX	390	13	52.0
19YY	488	14	70.0

In summary, Cdex will operate in a market defined by the intersection of two distinct trend lines. The first is the spread of microcomputer technology. That technology breeds a software vacuum which Cdex, as an electronic publisher, will attempt to fill. The total market for microcomputer programs in 19XX is estimated to be $1 billion. The second trend of interest is the increase in management and salespeople develpment, with an eye toward improved productivity. Cdex has a very favorable benefit-to-cost product story to sell into this market, which is estimated to be at least $488 million in in 19YY–$.5B in the diagram below.

Of the $1 billion microcomputer software market, an educated guess is that two thirds will be bought for business and professional applications ($660M). Of the $660M, perhaps 30 percent ($200M) will be for human resource development rather than accounting-related uses. Cdex expects to own 30-40 percent of that $200M market segment in 19YY for sales of $60-80M. The situation is summarized graphically below.

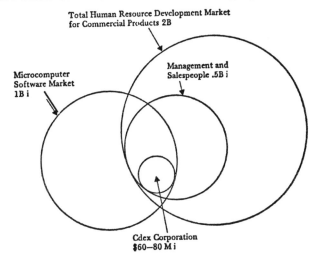

Total Human Resource Development Market
for Commercial Products 2B

Microcomputer
Software Market
1B i

Management and
Salespeople .5B i

Cdex Corporation
$60–80 M i

IV. PRODUCTION

There are six basic steps in the production process:
1. Capture quality subject matter on selected subjects
2. Program design
3. Program writing
4. Transfer of completed program into computer form (onto floppy disks)
5. Program validation
6. Program security, duplication, & distribution mechanics

Based on our experience to date in the production of high-quality Cdex programs, the allocation of time across the above is as follows:

10%	Subject matter acquisition
10%	Design
50%	Writing
20%	Programming
5%	Validation
5%	Mechanics
100%	

So far we have produced four programs:
XYZ Company Planning Process (ficticious co. name)
Perspective on Managing (#1 in catalog in Exhibit 1)
Stages of Company Growth (#2)
Basic Profit Math (#26)

The first program is currently in use in over fifty locations in the United States. The last three are the basis for the Cdex sales effort that will be initiated in early 19XX. Each program is approximately an hour in length in terms of participant running time. Our experience to date indicates that each program in our proprietary library will take us roughly 600-800 total hours to produce. Therefore, the forty initial programs planned (see Exhibit 1) will require over 20,000 person-hours to complete. Once a master disk is completed for a given program, additional disks (copies) will cost Cdex under $50 each (direct cost) for duplication and shipping.

The Cdex production process is dependent upon the PASS (Professional Authoring Software System) authoring program which we have licensed from Bell & Howell. The program enables Cdex authors to program quickly and efficiently once the subject material is in a structured, interactive format. Cdex is also licensed to resell copies of PASS to corporate customers interested in creating their own programs.

Bell & Howell currently has fifteen direct salespeople in the field selling PASS plus B&H microcomputers (private labeled from Apple). The activities of B&H are expected to be a plus for Cdex–both from a marketing and a production standpoint. In effect, B&H's success in the field will create a demand for Cdex proprietary programs. In addition, B&H's programming expertise will be of value to Cdex in such esoteric matters as encoding programs to prevent unauthorized duplication. Apple is also expected to be of help on this matter. To date, B&H's PASS customers include General Motors, Firemen's Fund, Standard Oil of Califomia, and Westinghouse.

Up to this point in time, Cdex has made the necessary capital expenditures to equip two programmers:

PASS License $30,000

Microcomputers (2) $10,000

Miscellaneous Equipment $5000

Over the next two years Cdex management expects to spend no more than $100,000 in total on office and program production capital expenditures. The production of proprietary Cdex programs is not capital intensive. The Cdex "secret" is in the conversion process, i.e., in capturing quality, proven subject matter and converting it via learning and computer technology into a new form, namely colorful, computer-assisted, interactive, interesting, multimedia instruction. Two members of the Cdex management and programming team are estimated be among the 100 most experienced people in the world in this conversion process insofar as it has been applied to more conceptual subjects such as those for management and salespeople development. (Most of the remaining 100 are with Control Data Corporation which has developed the PLATO system of interactive training using a CD mainframe computer.)

Knowledge of and skill in the conversion process (adaptation and reformatting of conceptual material) is relatively rare, and it lies at the heart of Cdex management's decision to position the company as an electronic *publisher* . . . rather than as a software producer of original material or a management training house. Within five to seven years, we expect to have 500-1,000 individual titles in our library covering a range of subjects of interest to "knowledge workers" (Peter Drucker's term) in the business and professional market.

From a staffing standpoint, program production will be concentrated in our Program Development Division (PDD) which will operate as a profit center after year two. We expect to have approximately nine programmers employed by 19XX with at least half of them working at home on Cdex-supplied microcomputers. Currently Cdex has one programmer full-time and another on call, a staffing level adequate to our current level of startup operation.

In general, we will develop our own programmers. We will use essentially the same approach for developing a core of three-to-four learning technologists–the people who must work in front of the programmers to break the subject (whatever it is) into an interesting, digestible, logically-sequenced series of frames with appropriate questions and responses and branches to insure learning. Cdex currently has a learning technologist on its staff for its initial library. By 19XX, we will have broadened our staff as necessary to handle new authors.

Currently Cdex management plans to approach a select group of proven authors to arrange for exclusive rights to the use of their materials in the Cdex computer-assisted format. Included in that group are:

[Names will be provided to prospective investors on request.]

Approaches to these authors will begin once Cdex financing is completed. We expect to operate on a royalty basis with signed authors, but on occasion may have to put some money "up front." In some respects Cdex will resemble a Twentieth-Century Fox which negotiates with authors for movie rights (different format) to certain proven books (e.g. *Superman)*.

In summary, the forty planned programs in the initial Cdex library are thought to be a relatively low-risk venture that will carry the company well over a third of the way to the $100 million sales mark by 19XX. Additional authors on additional proven topics (from setting up quality circles and EEO guidelines to decision making and working with Discounted Cash Flow) will be added systematically. In every case, Cdex will be utilizing a known and understood production process that reflects a unique, modern, relatively proprietary (Bell & Howell, Control Data, Deltak, and Cdex) combination of learning and computer technologies. Cdex will be the premier electronic publisher of human resource development products.

V. MARKETING

Smart marketing is the matter to which the Cdex top management [chief executive officer, chief operating officer] and board have given the most concentrated attention in the last few months. We believe we have developed a cost effective approach to the embryonic marketplace. IBM and HP's entries into the corporate market for personal computers tends to verify our line of thinking which can be summarized as follows:

Cdex will sell improved productivity, more effective management and salesmanship, and enhanced computer literacy to progressive United States companies via both direct sales effort and Cdex Training Centers in high density markets.

In general, our line of products will complement the efforts by Apple, Radio Shack, HP, IBM, etc. to sell personal computers. In general, our competition is the older, established purveyors of traditional human resource development products such as AMA (American Management Association), Louis Allen, Scientific Methods (Grid), industrial film companies like BNA and Roundtable, and the wave of seminar companies that have sprung up in recent years. In general, we will sell on a cost/benefit justification basis that contrasts the Cdex method of producing desired results with the alternatives. And in general, at least in the early years, we will sell a premium-priced product primarily to corporations rather than individuals. Details follow.

Product positioning. We identified twelve discrete positions around which we could weave our marketing effort.

They are as follows. Cdex early products could be promoted as:

1. Computer-assisted management and sales effectiveness improvers
2. Continuing education programs
3. A single, integrated–top management to supervisors–management development program
4. An MBA program for in-house use
5. A tested supervisory training program (There are currently 400 corporate users of the contents of Cdex programs numbered 11 through 20. See Exhibit 1.)
6. Basic ingredients for developing a "corporate culture," a phrase increasingly used in business circles
7. A strategic planning or strategic management series
8. Computer literacy enhancer (Provide a comfortable way for companies to introduce computers to their people.)
9. Productivity (or profitability) improvers
10. Building-block materials to supplement in-house development activities
11. Follow-on materials to live seminars based on Cdex products
12. Computer software

Given our pricing plans and our interest in developing a firm hold on the corporate market (see later), from the list we have decided to position Cdex products as:

9. Productivity improvers
1. Computer-assisted management & sales effectiveness improvers
8. Computer literacy enhancers

As a practical matter, we will also use #10 (Building blocks to supplement in-house efforts) as necessary–particularly when calling on corporate training directors. Alternatives #2, 3, 5, and 11 were passed as primary approaches because they led us toward becoming too subject-matter oriented. Also, these options lacked pizzazz. Alternatives #4, 6, and 7 were not, strictly speaking, technically complete, and the Cdex programs involved would not, by themselves, produce the results implied. Alternative #12 would carry us into a morass of low-priced, undifferentiated products that will be coming onto the market.

Our sense is that productivity and effectiveness are powerful, current themes for the corporate world, and they tie in with our plan to show that Cdex products are superior on a cost/benefit basis. Our sense is also that the personal computer publicity boom is going to create a demand for computer literacy to which Cdex's nonaccounting-oriented materials are a perfect answer.

Market segments. We identified eleven discrete segments that Cdex could pursue by various means. They were:

1. Fortune 1000 companies with established training budgets (Both the Cdex CEO and potential COO have reasonably good access to these companies.)
2. Smaller, technology-based, growth-oriented companies many of which already own personal computers
3. Bell & Howell customers (B&H has sold over $20 million of microcomputers upon which Cdex programs will run.)
4. Apple and IBM customers (Cdex programs run on Apple and IBM machines).
5. Training centers (Companies send individual managers, supervisors, or sales people to a nearby center.)
6. Individual consumers–typically people who already own personal computers
7. Selected vertical segments such as high-tech companies, banks, or retailing establishments
8. The professions, i.e., accounting, law, medicine, nursing
9. Government
10. Commercial schools, e.g., technician training, AMA, non-traditional MBA programs, etc.
11. Universities and colleges

Our thinking is that over the longer term, Cdex wants to be well established as *the* electronic publisher with a well-oiled distribution network to corporations. This point of view reflects the Cdex management team's interest, experience, and belief about where profit opportunity lies in the years ahead. Therefore, we have selected our segments accordingly with one proviso: We will concentrate on a geographic roll out (a form of segmentation) starting with west coast companies that are one or more of the following:

1. Fortune 1000
2. Smaller, growth companies
3. Bell & Howell customers

In addition, we will establish a Cdex Training Center in the geographic heart of Silicon Valley to which interested corporate customers can send individuals to take Cdex programs on a one-at-a-time basis. So add:

4. Training Centers

The other six segments have been rejected for the foreseeable future for a variety of reasons.

In summary, our targeted market is as follows:

I. Human resource development for productivity and effectiveness
    A. Business and professional "knowledge workers"
        1. Corporate purchasers–primarily manufacturers
            a. Large and higher growth companies that reside in high population density areas
                i. West Coast-NY/Boston-Atlanta-DFW-Houston

And we will solicit these targeted segments via direct sales efforts and Cdex Training Centers.

Product features. Cdex management feels that Cdex programs, used singly or in a series (see the matrix in Exhibit 1), offer the following, quantifiable benefits to corporate users:

1. Ease of administration. Programs are not instructor-dependent and can be used/scheduled twenty-four hours a day in one or more locations. In short, the programs are *need driven* –as opposed to schedule driven.

2. Consistent quality. With a Cdex program, management knows precisely what each participant gets–today, tomorrow, and beyond–in every part of the company. All members of the management or sales team, therefore, can sing from the same sheet of music, so to speak.

3. Consistent message. The people promoted or hired next week (month, year) get the same basic instruction that their predecessors did. This is the basis for synergism in a company.

4. Low cost per person, per program. For any repetitive development need, Cdex will be less expensive than any alternative (meetings, manuals, memos, off-site seminars, etc.). Cdex is aiming at a $10/person/ program objective by its fifth year. (See Pricing later.)

5. Superior subject recall and application. The benefits of the Cdex methodology were covered in Section I.

6. Flexibility. Cdex self-instructional programs can be integrated with virtually any other human resource development approach. For example, a sequence of Cdex programs can be periodically reviewed on a group basis. An instructor (or, better yet, a line manager) using a Cdex Review Session Leader's Guide can lead a provocative review session based on the material in the program.

7. Technology interface. To the extent that "the medium is the message," companies using personal computers to upgrade their people are conveying an upbeat, on-top-of-it image for the days ahead.

8. Pedigreed material. Each subject in the Cdex library is based, once again, on proven material, i.e., it has worked in the field. Cdex pulls together the best from academia and the real world of actual practice.

The details of precisely how these features will be fabricated into selling aids and advertising/promotion material will be worked out as the scheduled marketing talent is added to the Cdex team.

Pricing. Cdex management has examined in depth two major issues regarding pricing. First was whether to sell programs outright or license them for specific time periods (like a year) as a small gesture to keep control of the material. Second was whether to sell programs for a fixed figure or to sell them on a per-participant basis. Our conclusion is that we should sell them outright (rather than license them), and that we should sell them outright on the basis of the possible number of users in the buying organization.

Our long-term objective is to arrive at a point where we can sell programs based on a $10-per-participant, per-program basis. One participant taking one program is equivalent to what we call one Cdex Unit (1 CU). Roughly, our pricing schedule for 19XX through 19XX is as follows:

19XX	19XZ
$29/CU	$25/CU

Here is how the planned pricing will work. If Company X has 900 people in supervision and management and plans to buy the ten-program supervisory training series, the total price in 19XX would be $29 x 900 x 10 = $261,000. For this figure, Cdex would provide ten complete personal computers and ten copies of each of the ten programs . . . so Company X would have the equivalent of ten complete training "stations." (In 19XX, we will provide one station for each $25,000 purchase . . . or give credit to those who already own the necessary equipment.)

Another example, Company Y has forty salespeople and wishes to purchase five Cdex programs.

$$\$29 \times 40 \times 5 = \$5,800$$

We would provide no hardware in this instance.

We recognize the weakness in this per-participant approach, namely trying to get a fair initial price. It may be that we will have to establish a minimum price per program. A figure between $1,500 and $1,900 is being discussed by the Cdex board.

Sales. We are currently executing the second of a four-phase sales effort. Phase I took place between April and October of 19XX during which time the Cdex CEO exposed (in a nonselling mode) the first four completed programs to approximately 300 decision makers. Two hundred were in a local executive continuing education program; the other 100 were potential customers or investors, or both. The overwhelming response was positive interest that far exceeded mere curiosity. This business plan reflects much of the feedback received. Approximately $30,000 in sales were generated during this period.

Phase II, a direct personal selling effort by the CEO and potential chief operating officer (COO), was launched in mid-November and is aimed at signing on at least one major customer who will, in part, dictate which programs in the initial Cdex library will be produced next. We are quoting a figure of $10,000 per program (one-time charge) for which the customer receives programs featuring the buying company's name in the title (cosmetic customizing) plus publicity.

Phase III will begin with the addition of the COO full-time at which point he will simultaneously a) seek additional major customers to help us complete the library, b) recruit vice-presidents for the Corporate and Cdex Training Center Divisions (we have candidates identified for each position), and c) initiate our campaign to add at least two key authors to the Cdex stable.

Phase IV will commence in the third or fourth quarter of 19XX, approximately three months after the vice-presidents are on board and oriented. Phase IV will consist of a coordinated direct selling effort in a specific region (probably northern or southern California) to sell both Cdex programs and/or utilization of the local Cdex Training Center.

Note: Our current thinking is that corporations will be charged a price of $35-$39 per person, per program (1 CU) for people scheduled into our Training Center. This is a 25 percent premium over the "buy" price, but it allows companies to keep their human resource development cost on a variable cost basis. This may be important if the economy continues to undulate.

As a result of our systematic selling effort, we plan to sell Cdex Units as follows:

Year	Sales–CU's
19XX	40,650
19XY	165,500
19XZ	720,000
19YX	1,657,500
19YY	3,605,500

Here are both the pricing expectations in graph form.

Cdex Corporation

In conclusion, the Cdex marketing effort has been formulated from the best information and advice reasonably available plus the extensive experience base of the board. Further refinements will be incorporated as we expand our base of direct field selling. We are well aware that program distribution is now a major challenge confronting the entire microcomputer industry. Cdex intends to be a leader in developing a profitable, pacesetting solution.

VI. ORGANIZATION

Work is well along to bring together a core of qualified, capable, interested people to build the company described in this plan. Almost since its conception, Cdex has had an active board. The CEO and COO (committed candidate) have been working together since June in collaboration on both operations and the development of this plan. The program production effort has gone smoothly due to the tenacity of our senior programmer. And candidates are in mind for both vice-president slots: Corporate Division and Training Center Division.

Below is the Cdex organization chart for the 19XX-19XY period.

The board currently consists of three members:

Brown: Chairman and CEO. Sixteen years experience directly related to Cdex business. Experienced CEO and management developer.

Smith: Venture Capitalist. Founder of early company in multimedia, "teaching machine" field. Wide experience with growing companies.

Jones: Currently an officer with a Fortune 100 company where he is responsible for capital budgeting and strategic planning. Is also an active director of a high-growth semiconductor company.

CDEX Organization Chart 9-31-XX Business Plan

The chart above outlines the basic concept for the development of Cdex. In practice, the management team will operate as a functional team with a single profit center through 19XX and into 19XY.

The management team currently consists of two people. Once the needed capital is committed, two additional line people will be added. This group of four is expected to suffice through 19XX. In 19XY, at least one functional officer (e.g. CFO or Controller) may be added. At a later point in time, managers for two additional divisions (Consumer Division and OEM Division) will be considered.

Here are the management positions:

Title/Name	Primary Responsibility	Secondary
CEO/Brown	Execution of this plan. Staffing + team building. Development of Cdex library of programs.	Marketing.
COO/A	Execution of the plan. Cdex profitability. Staff building. Managing the divisions. Negotiations with authors. Computer mfgrs. interface.	Finance. Communications technology.
VP-CORPORATE DIV	Sell 40K CUs in 19XX.Develop salesforce. Build customer base. Pricing.	Product line extensions. Build Training Center Div.
VP-TRAINING CENTER DIV.	Open TC #1 by early 19XY. Sell 5K CUs in 19XX-19XY. Build customer base.	P. R. Build links to ASTD. Assist Corporate Div. Assess consumer market.

Cdex has a committed candidate (A) for the position of president and COO. He is currently an officer of a blue chip company with extensive experience in data processing, communications, planning, capital budgeting, performance appraisal (of line managers), and corporate negotiations. He has a strong line management background which includes five years as president of a small computer company and ten years as a SVP of a major bank. He has participated fully in the preparation of this plan. A is forty-four years old and has a degree in physics as well as an MBA.

Cdex has active candidates for both the vice-president slots. The candidate for the Corporate Division is currently a senior account executive for a $100 million, New York-based, service company. She has a very, very strong record of success in selling to major companies. She is thirty-six and has a BS in engineering.

The candidate for VP, Training Center Division, is currently the vice president of marketing for a $30 million consumer products company in the Bay Area. He has a broad base of marketing and sales experience running back to three years with P & G. He also has a sound background in general management having spent five years in charge of two different smaller companies. This candidate is forty and has a BA and an MBA. Resumes of the management team—CEO, COO, and one VP candidate—are included in Exhibit 3.

There are two other key positions unique to Cdex that will require qualified people:

<u>Director, Program Production</u>

Primary responsibility will be to manage all aspects of the microcomputer and software development interface. This person will have computer expertise.

<u>Director, Programming</u>

Primary responsibility will be the application of modern learning technology to business, human resource development opportunities. This person will have learning technology expertise as well as microcomputer experience.

We expect to be able to attract experienced people from the Bay Area to fill these positions. Generally speaking, other than for the COO (and possibly one of the VPs), staffing for Cdex will be drawn from near the corporate headquarters.

Long-run Outlook. Following is a *rough* word picture of how Cdex is expected to look by about 19YZ. At that point in time the company will have five profit centers and annual sales in excess of $70 million.

Corporate Division. Sells Cdex products plus some others directly to corporations. Has forty-to-fifty direct sales people in field working out of five-to-six regional offices in the United States plus offices in London, Mexico City, and Hong Kong. The Cdex name is well known and respected in the corporate world. We are doing image advertising in the *Wall Street Journal.* Sales average $1,000,000 per salesperson per year. Total Sales = $40M; Gross Margin = 75 percent.

Training Center Division. Has twelve training centers in high density areas of the United States plus one in Mexico City (with fifty training rooms). Each center averages $IM sales per year . . . operating at about 65 percent of capacity. Centers are open ten-to-twelve hours a day. Total sales = $13M; Gross Margin = 90 percent.

Program Development Division. Primary responsibility is preparation and QC of Cdex programs. In addition, PDD takes on selective custom programming contracts . . . particularly when they are on generic subjects that can be packaged by Cdex for its proprietary library. Total Sales = $15M; Gross Margin = 40 percent.

Consumer Division. Sells Cdex products plus some others indirectly to small business people and consumers via a variety of methods. Has four pilot learning centers in shopping centers in NY, LA, Palo Alto, and Washington, D. C. Total Sales = $20M; Gross Margin = 60 percent.

Original Equipment Division. Sells Cdex products through microcomputer manufacturers. Total Sales = $6M; Gross Margin = 15 percent–much too low. But Cdex position here keeps company at forefront of continuing personal computer revolution.

VII. FINANCIALS

Since June 19XX management has developed several computer models of Cdex in an attempt to develop a realistic picture of the funding needs and performance of the company in the years ahead. We have settled on best-case and worst-case (most conservative) scenarios with 19XX shown by month, 19XY by quarters, and beyond by years. These two very detailed scenarios are in our computer and available for examination, explanation, and discussion to interested management team candidates and investors. The key numbers from the projections are on the following page (in millions):

Best Case	19XX	19XY	19XZ	19YX	19YY
Sales $	1.2	5.7	20.5	41.6	73.1
NPAT $	.04	1.1	5.2	10.6	19.7
ROS %*	3	20	25	26	27
Cumm Cash $	.18	.9	4.5	14.1	29.3
Worst Case					
Sales $	.4	1.5	2.9	4.3	7.5
NPAT $	(.1)	.2	.5	.8	1.7
ROS %	—	11	18	19	23
Cumm Cash $	.2	.2	.7	1.4	3.0

* ROS % = Return on Sales percentage

In reviewing these two cases, we offer several observations. First, there is a big difference between the two scenarios insofar as the top lines (sales) go. But it is our considered opinion that with precisely the right packaging and marketing of our library, Cdex can indeed fulfill its opportunity very quickly. It can catch on and explode along with the microcomputer business. On the other hand, training materials per se are historically not "exploders," and our intended, rational, cost/benefit sell can take time. The front-end investment ($300,000-500,000) is roughly the same in either case, and the returns (on sales, investment, and equity) are very attractive in both scenarios, as a discussion of our detailed, line-itemed budgets with interested parties will show. Cdex management is confident it can successfully pilot the company on an opportunistic course between the two extremes, with the Best Case being the more likely outcome.

A second observation is that Cdex is a high-margin business that holds promise of being essentially self funding once it is launched. The cost of goods sold is minimal; inventory requirements are relatively small; capital investments will be primarily for microcomputer equipment (as opposed to bricks and mortar); and the programming expense structure is highly variable in that it can be increased or decreased incrementally as necessary. This gives management a lot of flexibility to deal with the changing times.

A third observation is that the intrinsic value of the company does not show in the financial projections (particularly the balance sheets) because it is in the finished programs–a growing library of sophisticated, computer-assisted, development programs covering the great ideas in business management and selling. The true value of the programs will not be reflected in the inventory figures. This library, and therefore, Cdex, is expected to become a very saleable asset to a host of potential buyers ranging from traditional publishers to computer manufacturers and the new world of TV networks. This means it will be practical for investors to recoup their money with appropriate capital gains within a reasonable time period of four-to-six years.

A final observation is that the basic idea behind Cdex is readily expandable. Broader coverage of the corporate market, foreign language versions of our programs, more training centers, and new subject areas for the library are all extensions of the efforts outlined in this Business Plan.

In summary, we have detailed plans reflecting pricing, sales effort, staffing, production, and capital expenditures for Cdex. Management expects to aim for the best case and be alert to the need to proceed on the basis of the worst-case scenario. Since the company's inception in mid-19XX, the Cdex management has consistently met its plans at each step along the way. With the necessary funding and staff additions, it will continue to do so.

The current balance sheet of the company is approximately as follows:

Cash	$ 20,000	A/P	$ 5,000
A/R	0		
Fixed Assets	20,000	Debt	13,000
Programs (3)	150,000	Net Worth	172,000
	$190,000		$190,000

VIII. OWNERSHIP

This business plan provides the basis for the third round of financing for Cdex. The history of the financing of the company is as follows:

History	# Shares	Ave. $/Share	% Cdex	$ Cash Invested
Round I—June 19XX				
Brown	1,400,000 Common	.04	100	$56,000
Round II—Sept. 19XX				
Directors	65,000 Common	.50	4	$32,500
Round III—Current				
Investors	650,000 C. Pfd.	.78	30	$500,000

Summary Including Management Stock Options (COO and VP's):

Brown	1,400,000	54
Directors	65,000	3
Investors	650,000	25
Mgmt. Stock Options	485,000	18
	2,600,000	100%

At this time we wish to sell 650,000 shares of preferred stock that is convertible 1:1 into common stock. The offering price for the convertible preferred is $.78.

Exhibits

Cdex Corporation
Business Plan

Exhibit 1

The Cdex
Personal Computer Library

Answers to 7 Important Questions

1 What is the Cdex Library?
The Cdex Library is a collection of high quality, English language personal computer programs on managing and selling practices. The first programs in the Library were available to users in June, 19XX. Additional programs are being added each month.

2 What specific subjects are available?
Thirty of the initial forty programs deal with subjects of current importance to executives, managers, and supervisors in dynamic companies. Ten of the forty are on industrial selling subjects. Each program is designed to bring together the best *proven* material from leading business schools and from the real world of actual practice. The enclosed matrix shows the

forty titles classified in ten major series.

3 Why use Cdex programs in your company?
There's a famous saying that goes like this: "I know that half the money I spend on management development is wasted . . . but I don't know which half!" Cdex programs mold learning and computer technology into interactive, personal development experiences that essentially guarantee the application of the subject matter on the job. When *quality* subject matter is remembered and applied, much of the "half wasted" disappears. And since Cdex programs are self-instructional, self-pacing, and portable, they can be used when and where they are needed . . . either individually or as part of an instructor-led development effort. Cdex programs

are building blocks that can be configured to meet your specific needs.

4 What are the costs involved?
Generally speaking, program costs are a function of the number of users in your company. For example, a company with 100 people in management and supervision would pay approximately $2900 to purchase or license a Cdex program. Hardware costs are between $3000 and $4000. Cdex will provide the hardware free-of-charge to major Library users.

5 What support services does Cdex provide?
When a series of programs are purchased or licensed, Cdex will train your company's training coordinator at no additional cost. Cdex can also provide the PASS (Professional Authoring Software System) program and assistance if you wish to prepare custom, computer-assisted development programs in your own company.

6 Who are the Cdex authors?
Contracts have been and are

being made with recognized experts in subjects important to companies on the go.

For example, along with other programs, the core series of programs on strategic planning shown in the attached matrix are authored by Professor Steven C. Brandt of the Stanford Business School and are based on his book, *Strategic Planning in Emerging Companies.*

7 What next?
Personally sample the programs of interest. Then select for use in your company the configuration of materials that will give you the maximum payoff in the coming year.

Contact Cdex for assistance in bringing the new world of computer-assisted human resource development to your company.

Cdex Corporation

Exhibit 1 ... continued

**The Cdex
Personal Computer
Library**

1. **Perspective on Managing—** Managing vs. doing. How to study, improve and use managing practices appropriate to your level of responsibility.
2. **Stages of Company Growth** —Five major stages of growth and the associated crisis at each stage. How to handle each crisis.
3. **Setting Company Objectives**—Criteria for sound objectives. Areas in which objectives should be set. MBO pitfalls to avoid.
4. **Selecting Planning Units—** Why planning units are necessary in a company of any complexity. Criteria for units. How proper units facilitate a planning process.
5. **Managing the Planning Process**—Key ingredients to making plans that get implemented. How to avoid the once-a-year project syndrome.
6. **Selecting a Planning Technique**—Eight major planning techniques. How to pick and stick with the best one for your company.
7. **Basic Strategies for Building a Company—**Six generic, proven ways to grow an enterprise and the minimum requirements for success for each strategy.
8. **Organizational Structures for Building a Company—** Four basic structures (func-
tional to matrix) for carrying out a company strategy. Pitfalls to avoid in changing your structure.
9. **Productivity Fundamentals** —Methods improvements. Involving all your people. How to work smarter, not harder.
10. **Cultivating a Corporate Culture**—Importance of a common vocabulary, company rituals, and the various reward systems. How to internalize values that enhance plan implementation.
11. **Perspective on Supervising** —Supervising vs. doing. How to break old habits of individual success and start achieving planned results through others.
12. **Setting Your Objectives—** Monthly, quarterly, and longer-term objectives. Criteria for sound objectives. Areas in which to set objectives.
13. **Improving Productivity—** Locating improvement possibilities. Use of checklists. Involving others. Selling methods improvements up the line.
14. **Working with Individuals** —Why general rules don't work. How people differ. Recent trends in social values. Dealing successfully with individual differences.
15. **Solving Day-To-Day Problems**—Kinds of problems

you face. Sources of problems. Sources of solutions. A procedure for getting the best solutions.

16. **Giving Day-To-Day Instructions**—Problems you face in communicating. When to use oral and written instructions. How to get the results you want.

17. **Training Your People**—Common pitfalls to avoid. Problems new employees face. How to develop effective training experiences.

18. **Disciplining Your People**—Basic principles. Special issues of the times. How to discipline without trepidation.

19. **Delegating with Confidence**—Reasons managers and supervisors delegate poorly. Psychological hurdles to overcome. How to get the delegating habit.

20. **Questioning & Listening**—Basic types of questions and when to use them. How to listen with your whole self. Drawing the most out of your people.

21. **Motivating Your People**—Factors that motivate people and how those factors change. What motivates people today. How to "unlock" each of your people individually.

22. **Evaluating Individual Performance**—Measuring activity, effort, appearances, and results. How to let people know how they are doing.

23. **Counseling Your People**—Problems people face. Signals to recognize. When to take action. How to help your people help themselves.

24. **Building a Career in Managing**—Factors for continuing success. Understanding managing. Setting realistic personal objectives. How to realize your ambitions.

25. **Planning Your Time**—Major time sumps. Setting priorities. Sticking with priorities. How to allocate your energies for maximum impact.

26. **Basic Profit Math**—A graphic approach that integrates marketing, production, and accounting. Break-even analysis. Effect of changing product mix. How to use BPM in planning.

27. **Ten Commandments for Growing a Company**—Key, proven principles for managing startups and young companies. Author is experienced entrepreneur and executive.

28. **Guide to Writing a Business Plan**—Concept, market opportunity, production, marketing, people, cash flow, and ownership. How to present your idea to investors.

29. **Developing a Competitive Advantage**—Four basic ways to excell in a chosen marketplace. How to cultivate your proprietary edge.

30. **Evaluating Company Performance**—Range of evaluation techniques: EPS, ROS, ROI, ROE, etc. Key

Exhibit 1 ... continued

factors to consider.

31. **Analyzing a Territory—** Key components for profitable growth. Getting the picture on competition. How to reach strategic conclusions.

32. **Working with Customers—** Why generalizations are dangerous. How people differ. Pressures customers face. How to tailor your approach to individual differences.

33. **Questioning & Listening to Sell—**Do you talk too much? Three basic types of questions. Maximizing the input from your customers.

34. **Selling in Writing—**When to use oral and written communications. Writing pitfalls to avoid. How to make your point on paper.

35. **Selling with Proposals—** Specifying the need. Laying out your solution. Formating. Action language. Closing. Followup.

36. **Thinking Creatively—**Selling solutions vs. selling products or services. Opening your mind. Opening the minds of others. Getting your message across.

37. **Understanding Profit Math** —Where sales dollars go. Product mix. Pricing. How to enhance your reputation as a businessperson.

38. **Setting Call Objectives—** Identifying the results you want. Analyzing the customer. What are the values involved? How to maximize your ROE (Return on Energy) each day.

39. **Conducting Group Meetings—**Setting objectives. Identifying the decision makers. Agendas. Presentation techniques. Effective wrap-ups.

40. **Overcoming Obstacles—** Common hurdles to effective closings. How to prempt problems. Questioning and listening to a committment. How to follow up.

Exhibit 2

The Cdex Personal Computer Library — Training Needs

Programs	Entrepreneuring	Managing the Emerging Company	Managing the Larger Company	Strategic Planning	Company Structure	Employee Productivity	Managing By Objectives	Supervising Subordinates	Strategic Selling (Industrial)	Personal Managing Skills
1. Perspective On Managing	•	•	•				•			•
2. Stages of Company Growth	•	•	•							•
3. Setting Company Objectives	•	•	•	•	•	•	•			
4. Selecting Planning Units		•	•	•	•					
5. Managing the Planning Process	•	•	•	•						
6. Selecting a Planning Technique		•	•	•						
7. Basic Strategies for Building a Company		•	•	•	•					
8. Organizational Structures for Building a Company	•	•		•	•		•			•
9. Productivity Fundamentals	•	•	•			•	•			
10. Cultivating a Corporate Culture	•	•	•	•	•					
11. Perspective on Supervising							•	•		•
12. Setting Your Objectives	•					•	•	•	•	
13. Improving Productivity						•		•		•
14. Working with Individuals	•	•					•	•		•
15. Solving Day-To-Day Problems							•	•		•
16. Giving Day-To-Day Instructions								•		•
17. Training Your People								•		
18. Disciplining Your People							•	•		
19. Delegating with Confidence	•							•		
20. Questioning & Listening	•					•		•		•

Exhibit 2 ... continued

The Cdex Personal Computer Library

Training Needs

Programs	Managing Personal Skills	Strategic Selling (Industrial)	Supervising Subordinates	Managing By Objectives	Employee Productivity	Company Structure	Strategic Planning	Managing the Larger Company	Managing the Emerging Company	Entrepreneuring
21. Motivating Your People			•							•
22. Evaluating Individual Performance	•	•	•	•					•	
23. Counseling Your People			•							
24. Building a Career in Managing	•		•							
25. Planning Your Time		•							•	•
26. Basic Profit Math		•		•	•	•			•	•
27. Ten Commandments for Growing a Company										•
28. Guide to Writing a Business Plan		•								•
29. Developing a Competitive Advantage		•						•	•	•
30. Evaluating Company Performance		•		•				•	•	•
31. Analyzing a Territory	•	•								
32. Working with Customers		•								
33. Questioning & Listening to Sell		•								
34. Selling in Writing		•								
35. Selling with Proposals		•								
36. Thinking Creatively		•								•
37. Understanding Profit Math	•	•	•							
38. Setting Call Objectives		•		•	•					
39. Conducting Group Meetings	•	•								
40. Overcoming Obstacles	•	•								•

Exhibit 3

RESUME

R.B. Brown
(Chairman & CEO)

Employment Background

● President, U.S. Management Development Corporation. Co-founded company and directed company growth to $16 million in sales. Negotiated successful sale of company to large, service-oriented conglomerate.

● V.P., Human Resources Development at General United Corporation (Fictitious name), a Fortune 500 company. Responsible for all phases of training, development and personnel.

● V.P., and General Manager of ABC Film Productions. Responsible for all programming and production. Profit responsibility included all phases of capital and expense budgeting at locations around the world. Company sales volume exceeded $40 million.

● Officer, U.S. Coast Guard.

Education

BSME, Purdue University, 1
MBA, Golden Gate University, 1

Personal

Married, two children. Mountain Climber.

Exhibit 3 ... continued

CONFIDENTIAL

RESUME

W.L. Cliffton
(Candidate for President & COO Position)

Employment Background

- Vice President—Planning, National American Company, a leading ($2B sales) competitor in the office equipment industry. Responsible for budgeting and all phases of strategy development.

- President, Calcutronics Computer Corporation, a $60 million manufacturer of military systems.

- Senior Vice President, First National Bank of Los Angeles. Responsibilities included (at various times) data processing, marketing, and commercial lending.

Education

BA, University of Virginia.
MBA, University of California
Southwestern Banking School, Southern Methodist University

Personal

Married. Jogger. Two books published.

Exhibit 3 ... continued

RESUME

Alice J. Fargo
(Candidate for Vice President—
Corporate Division)

Employment Background

- Senior Account Executive, LDI, Inc., a $100 million service company which provides economic forecasting to major companies. Progressed from position as sales representative to point where now responsible for over $4 million in annual revenues from a base of twenty-three clients.

- Sales Representative, IBM. Responsible for business products in Atlanta market.

- Customer Service Manager, A–M International in Chicago.

Education

BSEE, MIT

Personal

Peace Corps, Knitter

Epilog to
Appendix C

Venture Capitalists' Comments
on the Cdex Corporation
Business Plan

Ten professional venture capitalists reviewed the plan upon the request of the Cdex founders. Seven were from the west coast; two were from Chicago; one was New York City based. Five of the ten asked to see the detailed, confidential, financial plans that the Cdex management had developed. Following is a synopsis of the comments by the ten potential investors.

STRENGTHS

"Strong concept."

"Management appears to be balanced and appropriate for the business."

"Technology and timing look good."

"Understanding of production seems O.K."

"Market looks big . . . but hard to get to."

"Interesting idea. Pricing seems realistic."

"Programs are fantastic!"

"Training centers make a lot of sense."

"You're right. Micros are here to stay."

"Amazing gross margins."

"Excellent content in sample programs."

WEAKNESSES

"Distribution of finished products looks very messy. Very expensive."

"We don't like the marketing risk."

"Don't believe the sales projections (too high, too soon)."

"Too many unknowns in the training market."

"It's software. We don't invest in software. Only products."

"Price (for stock) is too high."

"You lack an experienced salesman at the top."

"I don't understand the business."

"You'll get drawn into custom programming—a service business."

"Weak linkage with Bell & Howell."

"Lacks analysis of competition—people like McGraw-Hill, Addison-Wesley, Apple Computer."

"No ROI information."

"Don't know of anyone who ever made money in the training business."

"Incomplete management team."

Of the ten potential investors, six said they were not interested ("no"). Most of these six indicated that Cdex just didn't fit their investment criteria. Cdex founders felt that there was a strong predisposition against "software" of any kind in this group.

Three of the remaining ten showed some interest. It varied from one firm's idea of hooking Cdex up with an existing company (in which the firm had an investment) that already had a program distribution network to another firm's request to be recontacted once several hundred thousand dollars in sales volume had been reached. This group seemed to smell an opportunity, but they were leery of the marketing/distribution challenges facing Cdex.

At the time this is being written, Cdex founders are still working with one of the ten potential investors. This particular investor has some personal background in publishing and human resource development. Together, the Cdex CEO and the venture capitalist are exploring several possible ways to "solve" the marketing/distribution issue at a reasonable cost. They currently share the view that Cdex can become a profitable $25,000,000 company in three-to-five years with an investment of under $1,000,000 and perhaps some selected additions to the product line and management team.

Author's Note: Cdex eventually raised over $1,000,000 in start-up capital based on a somewhat revised business plan and the addition of two senior people to the management team.

How to order Books & Videos
from Archipelago Publishing

We hope you found *Entrepreneuring: The Ten Commandments for Building a Growth Company* useful and helpful in building your business. If you have a business associate or relative who would benefit from having a copy of this book, here's how to order:

Single Copies
Please complete the ORDER FORM and mail or fax it to us. To order by phone, call toll free, 1-800-360-6166, 24 hours a day.

Quantity Orders
If you would like to distribute our books in your business or organization, or to your customers and clients as value-adding premiums, please call us immediately! Let us know how many copies you want, and we'll be happy to complete an order for you. We offer a substantial discount on orders of 25 or more books.

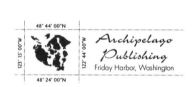

Archipelago Publishing
Build Your Business Guides
P.O. Box 1249
Friday Harbor, WA 98250
1-800-360-6166
Fax: 360-378-7097 • email: info@gmex.com

Build Your Business Guides
For more information about our *Build Your Business Guides* series, visit our website at **http://www.gmex.com**. There you will find excerpts from our books & videos, links to selected business resources, and other materials to help you build your business.

Archipelago Publishing
Friday Harbor, Washington

48° 44' 00"N
123° 15' 00"W
122° 44' 00"W
48° 24' 00"N

ORDER FORM

To order copies of this book or other business-building materials, complete this form and send or FAX it to:

Archipelago Publishing
Build Your Business Guides
P.O. Box 1249
Friday Harbor, WA 98250
FAX#360-378-7097

ORDER BY PHONE TOLL FREE!
1-800-360-6166

Quantity Discounts Available

YES! Please send me the following books or videos:

Qty	Title/Item#	Amount

TOTAL	_____
(WA State Residents add 7.7% Sales Tax)	_____
Shipping (see below)	_____
TOTAL DUE:$	_____

SHIP TO:

NAME:_____

ADDRESS:_____

CITY:_____ST:_____ ZIP:_____

DAYTIME PHONE:(   ) _____
(important)

Shipping Charges:
Book Rate: $2.00 for the first book and .75 for each additional book.
Priority Mail/First Class: $3.00 for up to three books.
Videos: $2.50 per video, or $15.00 for the series.

Payment:
Check Enclosed in the amount of $_____
Credit Card Orders: Visa or MasterCard Only

Card#_____ ex date:___/___

Signature:_____
Print Your Name:_____

For more information about any of our products & services, call
1-800-360-6166 or visit our website at http://www.gmex.com

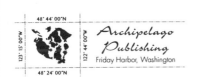

Archipelago Publishing
Friday Harbor, Washington

ORDER FORM

To order copies of this book or other business-building materials, complete this form and send or FAX it to:

Archipelago Publishing
Build Your Business Guides
P.O. Box 1249
Friday Harbor, WA 98250
FAX#360-378-7097

**ORDER BY PHONE
TOLL FREE!
1-800-360-6166**

Quantity Discounts Available

YES! Please send me the following books or videos:

Qty	Title/Item#	Amount

TOTAL _____
(WA State Residents add 7.7% Sales Tax)_____
Shipping (see below)_____
TOTAL DUE:$_____

SHIP TO:

NAME:_____

ADDRESS:_____

CITY:_____ST:_____ ZIP:_____

DAYTIME PHONE:(   ) _____
(important)

Shipping Charges:
Book Rate: $2.00 for the first book and .75 for each additional book.
Priority Mail/First Class: $3.00 for up to three books.
Videos: $2.50 per video, or $15.00 for the series.

Payment:
Check Enclosed in the amount of $_____
Credit Card Orders: Visa or MasterCard Only

Card#_____ ex date:___/___

Signature:_____
Print Your Name:_____

For more information about any of our products & services, call
1-800-360-6166 or visit our website at http://www.gmex.com

BUILD YOUR BUSINESS
YOUR
BUSINESS
GUIDES

BUILD YOUR BUSINESS NEWSLETTER

Stay on Top! We'll keep you informed of new products,
publications, and activities, along with seminar
announcements and other valuable information that
can help you build your business!

Please take a moment to send us your address, OR
visit our website at http://www.gmex.com and
complete the registration page.

YES! Please send me the Build Your Business Newsletter!

Name:_____

Company:_____

Address:_____

City:_____St:_____Zip:_____

email:_____

Phone:_____

Fax:_____

Return this form to:
Build Your Business Newsletter
Archipelago Publishing
P.O. Box 1249
Friday Harbor, WA 98250

For immediate information about Build Your Business
products and services, or to connect to our fax-on-
demand service, call us at 1-800-360-6166